STUDENT COMPANION BOOK TO ACCOMPANY
ADVANCED ACCOUNTING, 8E

Paul Marcus Fischer, PhD, CPA

Professor of Accounting

University of Wisconsin, Milwaukee

William James Taylor, PhD, CPA, CVA

Assistant Professor of Accounting

University of Wisconsin, Milwaukee

Rita Hartung Cheng, PhD, CPA

Associate Professor of Accounting

University of Wisconsin, Milwaukee

SOUTH-WESTERN

THOMSON LEARNING

Australia · Canada · Mexico · Singapore · Spain · United Kingdom · United States

SOUTH-WESTERN
™
THOMSON LEARNING

Student Companion Book
to Accompany
Advanced Accounting, 8e
Paul M. Fischer, William J. Taylor, Rita H. Cheng

Editor-in-Chief:
Jack W. Calhoun

Team Leader:
Melissa S. Acuña

Acquisitions Editor:
Sharon Oblinger

Developmental Editor:
Sara E. Wilson

Marketing Manager:
Jennifer L. Codner

Production Editor:
Heather A. Mann

Manufacturing Coordinator:
Doug Wilke

Production House:
Litten Editing and Production, Inc.

Compositor:
GGS Information Services, Inc.

Printer:
West Group
Eagan, MN

Design Project Manager:
Rik Moore

Internal Designer:
Craig Ramsdell, Ramsdell Design

Cover Designer:
Rik Moore

Cover Images:
PhotoDisc, Inc.
Digital Vision

For permission to use material from
this text or product, contact us by
Tel (800) 730-2214
Fax (800) 730-2215
http://www.thomsonrights.com

0-324-12261-6

CONTENTS

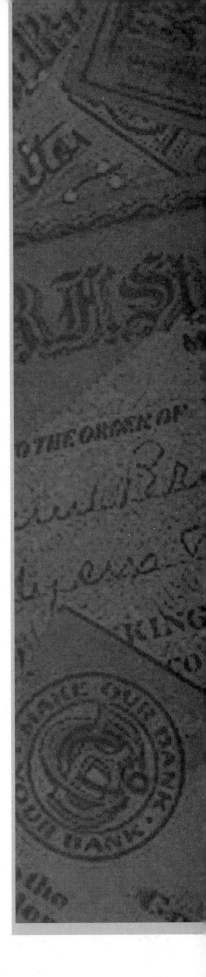

Worksheet 2-1

100% Interest; Price Equals Book Value
Company P and Subsidiary Company S
Worksheet for Consolidated Balance Sheet
December 31, 20X1

Worksheet 2-1 (see page 2-7)

	Trial Balance		Eliminations & Adjustments		Consolidated Balance Sheet	
	Company P	Company S	Dr.	Cr.		
1 Cash	300,000				300,000	1
2 Accounts Receivable	300,000	200,000			500,000	2
3 Inventory	100,000	100,000			200,000	3
4 Investment in Company S	500,000			(EL) 500,000		4
5						5
6 Equipment (net)	150,000	300,000			450,000	6
7 Goodwill						7
8 Current Liabilities	(150,000)	(100,000)			(250,000)	8
9 Bonds Payable	(500,000)				(500,000)	9
10 Common Stock—Company S		(200,000)	(EL) 200,000			10
11 Retained Earnings—Company S		(300,000)	(EL) 300,000			11
12 Common Stock—Company P	(100,000)				(100,000)	12
13 Retained Earnings—Company P	(600,000)				(600,000)	13
14 Totals	0	0	500,000	500,000	0	14

Eliminations and Adjustments:

(EL) Eliminate the investment in the subsidiary against the subsidiary equity accounts.

Worksheet 2-2

100% Interest; Price Exceeds Book Value
Company P and Subsidiary Company S
Worksheet for Consolidated Balance Sheet
December 31, 20X1

Worksheet 2-2 (see page 2-9)

	Trial Balance		Eliminations & Adjustments		Consolidated Balance Sheet	
	Company P	Company S	Dr.	Cr.		
1 Cash	100,000				100,000	1
2 Accounts Receivable	300,000	200,000			500,000	2
3 Inventory	100,000	100,000	(D1) 20,000		220,000	3
4 Investment in Company S	700,000			(EL) 500,000		4
5				(D) 200,000		5
6 Equipment (net)	150,000	300,000	(D2) 100,000		550,000	6
7 Goodwill			(D3) 80,000		80,000	7
8 Current Liabilities	(150,000)	(100,000)			(250,000)	8
9 Bonds Payable	(500,000)				(500,000)	9
10 Common Stock—Company S		(200,000)	(EL) 200,000			10
11 Retained Earnings—Company S		(300,000)	(EL) 300,000			11
12 Common Stock—Company P	(100,000)				(100,000)	12
13 Retained Earnings—Company P	(600,000)				(600,000)	13
14 Totals	0	0	700,000	700,000	0	14

Eliminations and Adjustments:

(EL) Eliminate the investment in the subsidiary against the subsidiary equity accounts.
(D) Distribute $200,000 excess of cost over book value as follows:
(D1) Inventory, $20,000.
(D2) Equipment, $100,000.
(D3) Goodwill, $80,000.

Worksheet 2-3

100% Interest; Price Exceeds Market Value of Identifiable Net Assets

Acquisitions Inc. and Subsidiary Johnson Company
Worksheet for Consolidated Balance Sheet
December 31, 20X1

Worksheet 2-3 (see page 2-12)

	Trial Balance		Eliminations & Adjustments		Consolidated Balance Sheet	
	Aquisitions	Johnson	Dr.	Cr.		
Cash	51,000	0			51,000	1
Accounts Receivable	42,000	28,000			70,000	2
Inventory	95,000	40,000	(D1) 5,000		140,000	3
Investment in Johnson Company	360,000			(EL) 128,000		4
				(D) 232,000		5
Land	60,000	10,000	(D3) 40,000		110,000	6
Buildings	500,000	60,000	(D4) 40,000		600,000	7
Accumulated Depreciation	(50,000)	(20,000)			(70,000)	8
Equipment	60,000	30,000	(D5) 30,000		120,000	9
Accumulated Depreciation	(24,000)	(10,000)			(34,000)	10
Patent (net)		15,000	(D6) 15,000		30,000	11
Brand Name Copyright			(D7) 40,000		40,000	12
Goodwill			(D8) 63,000		63,000	13
Current Liabilities	(89,000)	(5,000)			(94,000)	14
Bonds Payable	(100,000)	(20,000)			(120,000)	15
Discount (premium)				(D2) 1,000	(1,000)	16
Common Stock—Johnson		(1,000)	(EL) 1,000			17
Paid-In Capital in Excess of Par—Johnson		(59,000)	(EL) 59,000			18
Retained Earnings—Johnson		(68,000)	(EL) 68,000			19
Common Stock—Acquisitions	(20,000)				(20,000)	20
Paid-In Capital in Excess of Par—Acquisitions	(480,000)				(480,000)	21
Retained Earnings—Acquisitions	(405,000)				(405,000)	22
Totals	0	0	361,000	361,000	0	23

Eliminations and Adjustments:

(EL) Eliminate investment in subsidiary against subsidiary equity accounts.
(D) Distribute $232,000 excess of cost over book value as follows:
(D1) Inventory, $5,000.
(D2) Premium on bonds payable ($1,000).
(D3) Land, $40,000.
(D4) Buildings, $40,000.
(D5) Equipment, $30,000.
(D6) Patent, $15,000.
(D7) Brand name copyright, $40,000.
(D8) Goodwill, $63,000.

Worksheet 2-4

100% Interest; Price Exceeds Fair Value of Priority Accounts
Acquisitions Inc. and Subsidiary Johnson Company
Worksheet for Consolidated Balance Sheet
December 31, 20X1

Worksheet 2-4 (see page 2-15)

	Trial Balance		Eliminations & Adjustments		Consolidated Balance Sheet	
	Aquisitions	Johnson	Dr.	Cr.		
Cash	51,000	0			51,000	1
Accounts Receivable	42,000	28,000			70,000	2
Inventory	95,000	40,000	(D1) 5,000		140,000	3
Investment in Johnson	210,000			(EL) 128,000		4
				(D) 82,000		5
Land	60,000	10,000	(D3) 22,600		92,600	6
Buildings	500,000	60,000	(D4) 12,160		572,160	7
Accumulated Depreciation	(50,000)	(20,000)			(70,000)	8
Equipment	60,000	30,000	(D5) 12,600		102,600	9
Accumulated Depreciation	(24,000)	(10,000)			(34,000)	10
Patent (net)		15,000	(D6) 4,560		19,560	11
Brand Name Copyright			(D7) 26,080		26,080	12
Goodwill			(D8) 0			13
Current Liabilities	(89,000)	(5,000)			(94,000)	14
Bonds Payable	(100,000)	(20,000)			(120,000)	15
Discount (premium)				(D2) 1,000	(1,000)	16
Common Stock—Johnson		(1,000)	(EL) 1,000			17
Paid-In Capital in Excess of Par—Johnson		(59,000)	(EL) 59,000			18
Retained Earnings—Johnson		(68,000)	(EL) 68,000			19
Common Stock—Acquisitions	(17,000)				(17,000)	20
Paid-In Capital in Excess of Par—Acquisitions	(333,000)				(333,000)	21
Retained Earnings—Acquisitions	(405,000)				(405,000)	22
Totals	0	0	211,000	211,000	0	23

Eliminations and Adjustments:

(EL) Eliminate investment in subsidiary against subsidiary equity accounts.
(D) Distribute $82,000 excess of cost over book value as follows:
(D1) Inventory, $5,000.
(D2) Premium on bonds payable ($1,000).
(D3) Land, $22,600.
(D4) Buildings, $12,160.
(D5) Equipment, $12,600.
(D6) Patent, $4,560.
(D7) Brand name copyright, $26,080.
(D8) No amount available for goodwill.

Worksheet 2-5

100% Interest; Price Is Less than Fair Value of Priority Accounts

Acquisitions Inc. and Subsidiary Johnson Company
Worksheet for Consolidated Balance Sheet
December 31, 20X1

Worksheet 2-5 (see page 2-17)

	Trial Balance		Eliminations & Adjustments		Consolidated Balance Sheet	
	Aquisitions	Johnson	Dr.	Cr.		
1 Cash	51,000	0			51,000	1
2 Accounts Receivable	42,000	28,000			70,000	2
3 Inventory	95,000	40,000	(D1) 5,000		140,000	3
4 Investment in Johnson	35,000		(D) 93,000	(EL) 128,000		4
5						5
6 Land	60,000	10,000		(D3) 10,000	60,000	6
7 Buildings	500,000	60,000		(D4) 40,000	520,000	7
8 Accumulated Depreciation	(50,000)	(20,000)			(70,000)	8
9 Equipment	60,000	30,000		(D5) 20,000	70,000	9
10 Accumulated Depreciation	(24,000)	(10,000)			(34,000)	10
11 Patent (net)		15,000		(D6) 15,000		11
12 Brand Name Copyright			(D7) 0			12
13 Goodwill						13
14 Current Liabilities	(89,000)	(5,000)			(94,000)	14
15 Bonds Payable	(100,000)	(20,000)			(120,000)	15
16 Discount (premium)			(D2) 1,000		(1,000)	16
17 Common Stock—Johnson		(1,000)	(EL) 1,000			17
18 Paid-In Capital in Excess of Par—Johnson		(59,000)	(EL) 59,000			18
19 Retained Earnings—Johnson		(68,000)	(EL) 68,000			19
20 Common Stock—Acquisitions	(13,500)				(13,500)	20
21 Paid-In Capital in Excess of Par—Acquisitions	(161,500)				(161,500)	21
22 Retained Earnings—Acquisitions	(405,000)			(D8) 12,000	(417,000)	22
23 Totals	0	0	226,000	226,000	0	23

Eliminations and Adjustments:

(EL) Eliminate investment in subsidiary against subsidiary equity accounts.
(D) Distribute $93,000 excess of book value over cost as follows:
(D1) Inventory, $5,000.
(D2) Land, ($10,000).
(D3) Premium on bonds payable, ($1,000).
(D4) Building is eliminated; no value available.
(D5) Equipment is eliminated; no value available.

(D6) Patent is eliminated; no value available.
(D7) No amount available for brand name copyright.
(D8) No goodwill; record extraordinary gain. Since this is a balance sheet only, extraordinary gain is credited to retained earnings.

Worksheet 2-6

80% Interest; Price Exceeds Fair Value of Priority Accounts
Acquisitions Inc. and Subsidiary Johnson Company
Worksheet for Consolidated Balance Sheet
December 31, 20X1

Worksheet 2-6 (see page 2-20)

	Account	Trial Balance Acquisitions	Trial Balance Johnson	Eliminations & Adjustments Dr.	Eliminations & Adjustments Cr.	NCI	Consolidated Balance Sheet
1	Cash	51,000	0				51,000
2	Accounts Receivable	42,000	28,000				70,000
3	Inventory	95,000	40,000	(D1) 4,000			139,000
4	Investment in Johnson	290,000			(EL) 102,400 (D) 187,600		
5							
6	Land	60,000	10,000	(D3) 32,000			102,000
7	Buildings	500,000	60,000	(D4) 32,000			592,000
8	Accumulated Depreciation	(50,000)	(20,000)				(70,000)
9	Equipment	60,000	30,000	(D5) 24,000			114,000
10	Accumulated Depreciation	(24,000)	(10,000)				(34,000)
11	Patent (net)		15,000	(D6) 12,000			27,000
12	Brand Name Copyright			(D7) 32,000			32,000
13	Goodwill			(D8) 52,400			52,400
14	Current Liabilities	(89,000)	(5,000)				(94,000)
15	Bonds Payable	(100,000)	(20,000)				(120,000)
16	Discount (premium)				(D2) 800		(800)
17	Common Stock—Johnson		(1,000)	(EL) 800		(200)	
18	Paid-In Capital in Excess of Par—Johnson		(59,000)	(EL) 47,200		(11,800)	
19	Retained Earnings—Johnson		(68,000)	(EL) 54,400		(13,600)	
20	Common Stock—Acquisitions	(18,600)					(18,600)
21	Paid-In Capital in Excess of Par—Acquisitions	(411,400)					(411,400)
22	Retained Earnings—Acquisitions	(405,000)					(405,000)
23	Noncontrolling Interest					(25,600)	(25,600)
24	Totals	0	0	290,800	290,800	(25,600)	0

Eliminations and Adjustments:

(EL) Eliminate investment in subsidiary against 80% of the subsidiary's equity accounts.
(D) Distribute $187,600 excess of cost over book value as follows:
(D1) Inventory, $4,000.
(D2) Land, $32,000.
(D3) Premium on bonds payable, ($800).

(D4) Buildings, $32,000.
(D5) Equipment, $24,000.
(D6) Patent, $12,000.
(D7) Brand name copyright, $32,000.
(D8) Goodwill, $52,400.

Worksheet 2-7

80% Purchase, Bargain
Acquisitions Inc. and Subsidiary Johnson Company
Worksheet for Consolidated Balance Sheet
December 31, 20X1

Worksheet 2-7 (see page 2-23)

	Trial Balance		Eliminations & Adjustments		NCI	Consolidated Balance Sheet	
	Aquisitions	Johnson	Dr.	Cr.			
1 Cash	51,000	0				51,000	1
2 Accounts Receivable	42,000	28,000				70,000	2
3 Inventory	95,000	40,000	(D1) 4,000			139,000	3
4 Investment in Johnson	210,000			(EL) 102,400			4
5				(D) 107,600			5
6 Land	60,000	10,000	(D3) 26,480			96,480	6
7 Buildings	500,000	60,000	(D4) 23,168			583,168	7
8 Accumulated Depreciation	(50,000)	(20,000)				(70,000)	8
9 Equipment	60,000	30,000	(D5) 18,480			108,480	9
10 Accumulated Depreciation	(24,000)	(10,000)				(34,000)	10
11 Patent (net)		15,000	(D6) 8,688			23,688	11
12 Brand Name Copyright			(D7) 27,584			27,584	12
13 Goodwill			(D8) 0			0	13
14 Current Liabilities	(89,000)	(5,000)				(94,000)	14
15 Bonds Payable	(100,000)	(20,000)				(120,000)	15
16 Discount (premium)				(D2) 800		(800)	16
17 Common Stock—Johnson		(1,000)	(EL) 800		(200)		17
18 Paid-In Capital in Excess of Par—Johnson		(59,000)	(EL) 47,200		(11,800)		18
19 Retained Earnings—Johnson		(68,000)	(EL) 54,400		(13,600)		19
20 Common Stock—Acquisitions	(17,000)					(17,000)	20
21 Paid-In Capital in Excess of Par—Acquisitions	(333,000)					(333,000)	21
22 Retained Earnings—Acquisitions	(405,000)					(405,000)	22
23 Noncontrolling Interest					(25,600)	(25,600)	23
24 Totals	0	0	210,800	210,800	(25,600)	0	24

Eliminations and Adjustments:

(EL) Eliminate investment in subsidiary against 80% of the subsidiary's equity accounts.
(D) Distribute $107,600 excess of cost over book value as follows:
(D1) Inventory, $4,000.
(D2) Premium on bonds payable, ($800).
(D3) Land, $26,480.

(D4) Buildings, $23,168.
(D5) Equipment, $18,480.
(D6) Patent, $8,688.
(D7) Brand name copyright, $27,584.

Worksheet 3-1

Simple Equity Method
Company P and Subsidiary Company S
Worksheet for Consolidated Financial Statements
For Year Ended December 31, 20X1

	(Credit balance amounts are in parentheses.)	Trial Balance	
		Company P	Company S
1	**Investment in Company S**	**163,000**	
2			
3			
4	**Patent**		
5	Other Assets (net of liabilities)	227,000	170,000
6	Common Stock ($10 par), Company P	(200,000)	
7	Retained Earnings, Jan. 1, 20X1, Company P	(123,000)	
8	Common Stock, ($10 par) Company S		(100,000)
9	Retained Earnings, Jan. 1, 20X1, Company S		(50,000)
10	Revenue	(100,000)	(80,000)
11	**Expenses**	60,000	50,000
12	**Patent Amortization**		
13	**Subsidiary Income**	**(27,000)**	
14	**Dividends Declared**		10,000
15		0	0
16	**Consolidated Net Income**		
17	**To NCI (see distribution schedule)**		
18	**Balance to Controlling Interest (see distribution schedule)**		
19	Total NCI		
20	Retained Earnings, Controlling Interest, Dec. 31, 20X1		
21			

Eliminations and Adjustments:

(CY1) Eliminate subsidiary income against the investment account.
(CY2) Eliminate dividends paid by subsidiary to parent. After (CY1) and (CY2), the investment account and subsidiary retained earnings are at a common point in time. Then, elimination of the investment account can proceed.
(EL) Eliminate the pro rata share of Company S equity balances *at the beginning of the year* against the investment account. The elimination of the parent's share of subsidiary stockholders' equity leaves only the noncontrolling interest in each element of the equity.
(D) Distribute the $10,000 excess cost as required by the D&D schedule on page 3-3. In this example, Patent is recorded for $10,000.
(A) Amortize the resulting patents over the 10-year period. The current portion is $1,000 per year ($10,000 ÷ 10 years).

Worksheet 3-1 (see page 3-5)

Eliminations & Adjustments				Consolidated Income Statement		NCI		Controlling Retained Earnings		Consolidated Balance Sheet	
Dr.		Cr.									
(CY2)	9,000	(CY1)	27,000								1
		(EL)	135,000								2
		(D)	10,000								3
(D)	10,000	(A)	1,000							9,000	4
										397,000	5
										(200,000)	6
								(123,000)			7
(EL)	90,000					(10,000)					8
(EL)	45,000					(5,000)					9
				(180,000)							10
				110,000							11
(A)	1,000			1,000							12
(CY1)	27,000										13
		(CY2)	9,000			1,000					14
	182,000		182,000								15
				(69,000)							16
				3,000		(3,000)					17
				66,000				(66,000)			18
						(17,000)				(17,000)	19
								(189,000)		(189,000)	20
										0	21

Subsidiary Company S Income Distribution

Internally generated net income	$ 30,000
Adjusted income	$ 30,000
NCI share	10%
NCI	**$ 3,000**

Parent Company P Income Distribution

Patent amortization . . . . (A)	**$1,000**	Internally generated net income	$40,000
		90% × Company S adjusted income of $30,000	27,000
		Controlling interest	**$66,000**

Worksheet 3-2

Simple Equity Method, Second Year
Company P and Subsidiary Company S
Worksheet for Consolidated Financial Statements
For Year Ended December 31, 20X2

	(Credit balance amounts are in parentheses.)	Trial Balance	
		Company P	Company S
1	Investment in Company S	149,500	
2			
3	Patent		
4	Other Assets (net of liabilities)	251,500	155,000
5	Common Stock ($10 par), Company P	(200,000)	
6	Retained Earnings, Jan. 1, 20X2, Company P	(190,000)	
7	Common Stock, ($10 par) Company S		(100,000)
8	Retained Earnings, Jan. 1, 20X2, Company S		(70,000)
9	Revenue	(100,000)	(50,000)
10	Expenses	80,000	60,000
11	Patent Amortization		
12	Subsidiary Loss	9,000	
13	Dividends Declared		5,000
14		0	0
15	Consolidated Net Income		
16	To NCI (see distribution schedule)		
17	Balance to Controlling Interest (see distribution schedule)		
18	Total NCI		
19	Retained Earnings, Controlling Interest, Dec. 31, 20X2		
20			

Eliminations and Adjustments:

(CY1) Eliminate controlling share of subsidiary loss.

(CY2) Eliminate dividends paid by subsidiary to parent. The investment account is now returned to its January 1, 20X2 balance so that elimination may proceed.

(EL) Using balances *at the beginning of the year*, eliminate 90% of the Company S equity balances against the remaining investment account.

(D) Distribute the $10,000 excess cost as indicated by the D&D schedule that was prepared on the date of acquisition.

(A) Amortize the patent over the selected 10-year period. It is necessary to record the amortization *for current and past periods*, because asset adjustments resulting from the consolidation process do not appear on the separate statements of the constituent companies. Thus, entry (A) reduces Patent by $2,000 for the 20X1 and 20X2 amortizations. The amount for the current year is expensed, while the cumulative amortization for prior years is deducted from the beginning controlling retained earnings account. The NCI does not share in the adjustments because the only patent originally acknowledged is that which is applicable to the controlling interest.

Worksheet 3-2 (see page 3-8)

Eliminations & Adjustments				Consolidated Income Statement	NCI	Controlling Retained Earnings	Consolidated Balance Sheet	
Dr.		Cr.						
(CY1)	9,000	(EL)	153,000					1
(CY2)	4,500	(D)	10,000					2
(D)	10,000	(A)	2,000				8,000	3
							406,500	4
							(200,000)	5
(A)	1,000					(189,000)		6
(EL)	90,000				(10,000)			7
(EL)	63,000				(7,000)			8
				(150,000)				9
				140,000				10
(A)	1,000			1,000				11
		(CY1)	9,000					12
		(CY2)	4,500		500			13
	178,500		178,500					14
				(9,000)				15
				(1,000)	1,000			16
				10,000		(10,000)		17
					(15,500)		(15,500)	18
						(199,000)	(199,000)	19
							0	20

Subsidiary Company S Income Distribution

Internally generated **loss**	$ 10,000
Adjusted income	$ 10,000
NCI share	10%
NCI	**$ 1,000**

Parent Company P Income Distribution

Patent amortization . . . . (A)	**$ 1,000**	Internally generated net income	$ 20,000
90% × Company S adjusted income of			
$10,000	9,000		
		Controlling interest	**$10,000**

Worksheet 3-3

Cost Method
Company P and Subsidiary Company S
Worksheet for Consolidated Financial Statements
For Year Ended December 31, 20X1

	(Credit balance amounts are in parentheses.)	Trial Balance	
		Company P	Company S
1	**Investment in Company S**	145,000	
2			
3	**Patent**		
4	Other Assets (net of liabilities)	227,000	170,000
5	Common Stock ($10 par), Company P	(200,000)	
6	Retained Earnings, Jan. 1, 20X1, Company P	(123,000)	
7	Common Stock, ($10 par) Company S		(100,000)
8	Retained Earnings, Jan. 1, 20X1, Company S		(50,000)
9	Revenue	(100,000)	(80,000)
10	Expenses	60,000	50,000
11	**Patent Amortization**		
12	**Subsidiary (Dividend) Income**	(9,000)	
13	**Dividends Declared**		10,000
14		0	0
15	Consolidated Net Income		
16	To NCI (see distribution schedule)		
17	Balance to Controlling Interest (see distribution schedule)		
18	Total NCI		
19	Retained Earnings, Controlling Interest, Dec. 31, 20X1		
20			

Eliminations and Adjustments:

(CY2) Eliminate intercompany dividends.
(EL) Eliminate 90% of the Company S equity balances at the beginning of the year against the investment account.
(D) Distribute the $10,000 excess cost as indicated by the D&D schedule on page 3-6.
(A) Amortize the patent for the current year.

Worksheet 3-3 (see page 3-10)

Eliminations & Adjustments					Consolidated Income Statement		NCI		Controlling Retained Earnings		Consolidated Balance Sheet		
Dr.		Cr.											
		(EL)	135,000										1
		(D)	10,000										2
(D)	10,000	(A)	1,000								9,000		3
											397,000		4
											(200,000)		5
									(123,000)				6
(EL)	90,000						(10,000)						7
(EL)	45,000						(5,000)						8
					(180,000)								9
					110,000								10
(A)	1,000				1,000								11
(CY2)	9,000												12
		(CY2)	9,000				1,000						13
	155,000		155,000										14
					(69,000)								15
					3,000		(3,000)						16
					66,000				(66,000)				17
							(17,000)				(17,000)		18
									(189,000)		(189,000)		19
											0		20

Subsidiary Company S Income Distribution

Internally generated net income	$ 30,000
Adjusted income	$ 30,000
NCI share	10%
NCI	**$ 3,000**

Parent Company P Income Distribution

Patent amortization . . . . (A)	$1,000	Internally generated net income	$ 40,000
		90% × Company S adjusted income of	
		$30,000	27,000
		Controlling interest	**$66,000**

Worksheet 3-4

Cost Method, Second Year
Company P and Subsidiary Company S
Worksheet for Consolidated Financial Statements
For Year Ended December 31, 20X2

	(Credit balance amounts are in parentheses.)	Trial Balance	
		Company P	Company S
1	**Investment in Company S**	145,000	
2			
3	Patent		
4	Other Assets (net of liabilities)	251,500	155,000
5	Common Stock ($10 par), Company P	(200,000)	
6	**Retained Earnings, Jan. 1, 20X2, Company P**	(172,000)	
7	Common Stock, ($10 par) Company S		(100,000)
8	Retained Earnings, Jan. 1, 20X2, Company S		(70,000)
9	Revenue	(100,000)	(50,000)
10	Expenses	80,000	60,000
11	Patent Amortization		
12	**Subsidiary (Dividend) Income**	(4,500)	
13	**Dividends Declared**		5,000
14		0	0
15	Consolidated Net Income		
16	To NCI (see distribution schedule)		
17	Balance to Controlling Interest (see distribution schedule)		
18	Total NCI		
19	Retained Earnings, Controlling Interest, Dec. 31, 20X2		
20			

Eliminations and Adjustments:

(CV) Convert to simple equity method as of January 1, 20X2.
(CY2) Eliminate the current year intercompany dividends.
(EL) Eliminate 90% of the Company S equity balances at the beginning of the year against the investment account.
(D) Distribute the $10,000 excess cost as indicated by the D&D schedule that was prepared on the date of acquisition.
(A) Amortize the patent for the current year and one previous year.

Worksheet 3-4 (see page 3-10)

Eliminations & Adjustments				Consolidated Income Statement	NCI	Controlling Retained Earnings	Consolidated Balance Sheet	
Dr.		Cr.						
(CV)	18,000	(EL)	153,000					1
		(D)	10,000					2
(D)	10,000	(A)	2,000				8,000	3
							406,500	4
							(200,000)	5
(A)	1,000	(CV)	18,000			(189,000)		6
(EL)	90,000				(10,000)			7
(EL)	63,000				(7,000)			8
				(150,000)				9
				140,000				10
(A)	1,000			1,000				11
(CY2)	4,500							12
		(CY2)	4,500		500			13
	187,500		187,500					14
				(9,000)				15
				(1,000)	1,000			16
				10,000		(10,000)		17
					(15,500)		(15,500)	18
						(199,000)	(199,000)	19
							0	20

Subsidiary Company S Income Distribution

Internally generated **loss**	$ 10,000
Adjusted income	$ 10,000
NCI share	10%
NCI	**$ 1,000**

Parent Company P Income Distribution

Patent amortization . . . . (A)	$1,000	Internally generated net income	$ 20,000
90% × Company S adjusted income of			
$10,000	9,000		
		Controlling interest	**$10,000**

Worksheet 3-5

Simple Equity Method, First Year
Paulos Company and Subsidiary Carlos Company
Worksheet for Consolidated Financial Statements
For Year Ended December 31, 20X1

	(Credit balance amounts are in parentheses.)	Trial Balance	
		Paulos	Carlos
1	Cash	100,000	50,000
2	Inventory	226,000	62,500
3	Land	200,000	150,000
4	Investment in Carlos	732,000	
5			
6			
7	Buildings	800,000	600,000
8	Accumulated Depreciation	(80,000)	(315,000)
9	Equipment	400,000	150,000
10	Accumulated Depreciation	(50,000)	(70,000)
11	Patent (net)		112,500
12	Goodwill		
13	Current Liabilities	(100,000)	
14	Bonds Payable		(200,000)
15	Discount (premium)		
16	Common Stock, Carlos		(100,000)
17	Paid-In Capital in Excess of Par, Carlos		(150,000)
18	Retained Earnings, Jan. 1, 20X1, Carlos		(250,000)
19	Common Stock, Paulos	(1,500,000)	
20	Retained Earnings, Jan. 1, 20X1, Paulos	(600,000)	
21	Sales	(350,000)	(200,000)
22	Cost of Goods Sold	150,000	80,000
23	Depr. Expense—Building	40,000	15,000
24	Depreciation Exp.—Equipment	20,000	20,000
25	Other Expenses	60,000	13,000
26	Interest Expense		12,000
27	Subsidiary Income	(48,000)	
28	Dividends Declared		20,000
29	Totals	0	0
30	Consolidated Net Income		
31	NCI Share		
32	Controlling Share		
33	Total NCI		
34	Retained Earnings, Controlling Interest, Dec. 31, 20X1		
35	Totals		

Worksheet 3-5 (see page 3-16)

Eliminations & Adjustments				Consolidated Income Statement	NCI	Controlling Retained Earnings	Consolidated Balance Sheet	
Dr.		Cr.						
							150,000	1
							288,500	2
(D2)	40,000	(CY1)	48,000				390,000	3
(CY2)	16,000							4
		(EL)	400,000					5
		(D)	300,000					6
(D4)	160,000						1,560,000	7
		(A4)	8,000				(403,000)	8
		(D5)	16,000				534,000	9
(A5)	3,200						(116,800)	10
(D6)	20,000							11
(D7)	81,400						81,400	12
							(100,000)	13
							(200,000)	14
(D3)	10,600	(A3)	2,650				7,950	15
(EL)	80,000				(20,000)			16
(EL)	120,000				(30,000)			17
(EL)	200,000				(50,000)			18
							(1,500,000)	19
						(600,000)		20
				(550,000)				21
(D1)	4,000			234,000				22
(A4)	8,000			63,000				23
		(A5)	3,200	36,800				24
(A6)	2,000			75,000				25
(A3)	2,650			14,650				26
(CY1)	48,000							27
		(CY2)	16,000		4,000			28
	795,850		795,850					29
				(126,550)				30
				12,000	(12,000)			31
				114,550		(114,550)		32
					(108,000)		(108,000)	33
						(714,550)	(714,550)	34
							0	35

Eliminations and Adjustments:

(CY1) Eliminate current year entries made to record subsidiary income.
(CY2) Eliminate dividends paid by Carlos to Paulos. The investment is now at its January 1, 20X1 balance.
(EL)   Eliminate 80% of subsidiary equity against the investment account.
(D)   Distribute $300,000 excess as follows:
(D1)   Cost of goods sold for inventory adjustment at time of purchase.
(D2)   Land adjustment.
(D3)   Record discount on bonds payable..
(D4)   Adjust building.
(D5)   Adjust equipment.
(D6)   Adjust patent.
(D7)   Record goodwill.

(A3-6)	Account Adjustments To Be Amortized	Life	Annual Amount	Current Year	Prior Years	Total	Key
	Bonds payable	4	$ 2,650	$ 2,650	0	$ 2,650	(A3)
	Buildings	20	8,000	8,000	0	8,000	(A4)
	Equipment	5	(3,200)	(3,200)	0	(3,200)	(A5)
	Patent (net)	10	2,000	2,000	0	2,000	(A6)
	Total	0	$ 9,450	$ 9,450	0	$ 9,450	

Subsidiary Carlos Company Income Distribution

Internally generated net income	$ 60,000
Adjusted income	$ 60,000
NCI share	20%
NCI	$ 12,000

Parent Paulos Company Income Distribution

Amortizations of excess (Elim. A) . . . . (A3-6)	$9,450	Internally generated net income	$ 80,000
Inventory adjustment . . . . (D1)	4,000	80% × Carlos adjusted income	48,000
		Controlling interest	$114,550

Worksheet 3-6

Simple Equity Method, Second Year
Paulos Company and Subsidiary Carlos Company
Worksheet for Consolidated Financial Statements
For Year Ended December 31, 20X2

	(Credit balance amounts are in parentheses.)	Trial Balance	
		Paulos	Carlos
1	Cash	312,000	160,000
2	Inventory	210,000	120,000
3	Land	200,000	150,000
4	Investment in Carlos	796,000	
5			
6			
7	Buildings	800,000	600,000
8	Accumulated Depreciation	(120,000)	(330,000)
9	Equipment	400,000	150,000
10	Accumulated Depreciation	(90,000)	(90,000)
11	Patent (net)		100,000
12	Goodwill		
13	Current Liabilities	(150,000)	(40,000)
14	Bonds Payable		(200,000)
15	Discount (premium)		
16	Common Stock, Carlos		(100,000)
17	Paid-In Capital in Excess of Par, Carlos		(150,000)
18	Retained Earnings, Jan. 1, 20X2, Carlos		(290,000)
19	Common Stock, Paulos	(1,500,000)	
20	Retained Earnings, Jan. 1, 20X2, Paulos	(728,000)	
21			
22	Sales	(400,000)	(300,000)
23	Cost of Goods Sold	200,000	120,000
24	Depr. Expense—Building	40,000	15,000
25	Depreciation Exp.—Equipment	20,000	20,000
26	Other Expenses	90,000	33,000
27	Interest Expense		12,000
28	Subsidiary Income	(80,000)	
29	Dividends Declared		20,000
30	Totals	0	0
31	Consolidated Net Income		
32	NCI Share		
33	Controlling Share		
34	Total NCI		
35	Retained Earnings, Controlling Interest, Dec. 31, 20X2		
36	Totals		

Worksheet 3-6 (see page 3-17)

Eliminations & Adjustments				Consolidated Income Statement	NCI	Controlling Retained Earnings	Consolidated Balance Sheet	
Dr.		Cr.						
							472,000	1
							330,000	2
(D2)	40,000						390,000	3
(CY2)	16,000	(CY1)	80,000					4
		(EL)	432,000					5
		(D)	300,000					6
(D4)	160,000						1,560,000	7
		(A4)	16,000				(466,000)	8
		(D5)	16,000				534,000	9
(A5)	6,400						(173,600)	10
(D6)	20,000	(A6)	4,000					11
(D7)	81,400						81,400	12
							(190,000)	13
							(200,000)	14
(D3)	10,600	(A3)	5,300					15
(EL)	80,000				(20,000)			16
(EL)	120,000				(30,000)			17
(EL)	232,000				(58,000)			18
							(1,500,000)	19
(D1)	4,000							20
(A3-6)	9,450					(714,550)		21
				(700,000)				22
				320,000				23
(A4)	8,000			63,000				24
		(A5)	3,200	36,800				25
(A6)	2,000			125,000				26
(A3)	2,650			14,650				27
(CY1)	80,000							28
		(CY2)	16,000		4,000			29
	872,500		872,500					30
				(140,550)				31
				20,000	(20,000)			32
				120,550		(120,550)		33
					(124,000)		(124,000)	34
						(835,100)	(835,100)	35
							0	36

Eliminations and Adjustments:

(CY1)   Eliminate current year entries made to record subsidiary income.
(CY2)   Eliminate dividends paid by Carlos to Paulos. The investment is now at its January 1, 20X2 balance.
(EL)   Eliminate 80% of subsidiary equity against the investment account.
(D)   Distribute $300,000 excess as follows:
(D1)   Cost of goods sold for inventory adjustment at time of purchase.
(D2)   Land adjustment.
(D3)   Record discount on bonds payable.
(D4)   Adjust building.
(D5)   Adjust equipment.
(D6)   Adjust patent.
(D7)   Record goodwill.

(A3-6)	Account Adjustments To Be Amortized	Life	Annual Amount	Current Year	Prior Years	Total	Key
	Bonds payable	4	$ 2,650	$ 2,650	$ 2,650	$ 5,300	(A3)
	Buildings	20	8,000	8,000	8,000	16,000	(A4)
	Equipment	5	(3,200)	(3,200)	(3,200)	(6,400)	(A5)
	Patent (net)	10	2,000	2,000	2,000	4,000	(A6)
	Total		$ 9,450	$ 9,450	$ 9,450	$18,900	

Subsidiary Carlos Company Income Distribution

	Internally generated net income	$100,000
	Adjusted income	$100,000
	NCI share	20%
	NCI	$ 20,000

Parent Paulos Company Income Distribution

Amortizations of excess (Elim. A) . . . . (A3-6)	$9,450	Internally generated net income	$ 50,000
		80% × Carlos adjusted income	80,000
		Controlling interest	$120,550

Worksheet 3-7

Intraperiod Purchase; Subsidiary Books Closed on Purchase Date
Company P and Subsidiary Company S
Worksheet for Consolidated Financial Statements
For Year Ended December 31, 20X1

	(Credit balance amounts are in parentheses.)	Trial Balance	
		Company P	Company S
1	Current Assets	187,600	87,500
2	**Investment in Company S**	**118,400**	
3			
4			
5	Goodwill		
6	Equipment	400,000	80,000
7	Accumulated Depreciation	(200,000)	(32,500)
8	Liabilities	(60,000)	(12,000)
9	Common Stock, Company P	(250,000)	
10	Retained Earnings, **Jan. 1, 20X1, Company P**	(100,000)	
11	Common Stock, Company S		(50,000)
12	Retained Earnings, **July 1, 20X1, Company S**		(58,000)
13	Sales	(500,000)	(92,000)
14	Cost of Goods Sold	350,000	60,000
15	Expenses	70,000	12,000
16	**Subsidiary Income**	**(16,000)**	
17	Dividends Declared		5,000
18			
19		0	0
20			
21	Consolidated Net Income		
22	To NCI (see distribution schedule)		
23	Balance to Controlling Interest (see distribution schedule)		
24	Total NCI		
25	Retained Earnings, Controlling Interest, Dec. 31, 20X1		
26			

Eliminations and Adjustments:

(CY1)   Eliminate the entries made in the investment in Company S account and in the subsidiary income account to record the parent's 80% controlling interest in the subsidiary's second *6-months' income.*
(CY2)   Eliminate intercompany dividends. This restores the investment account to its balance as of the July 1, 20X1 investment date.
(EL)   Eliminate 80% of the subsidiary's *July 1, 20X1* equity balances against the *balance* of the investment account.
(D)   Distribute the excess of cost over book value of $20,000 to Goodwill in accordance with the D&D schedule.

Worksheet 3-7 (see page 3-22)

Eliminations & Adjustments				Consolidated Income Statement	Minority Interest	Controlling Retained Earnings	Consolidated Balance Sheet	
Dr.		Cr.						
							275,100	1
(CY2)	4,000	(CY1)	16,000					2
		(EL)	86,400					3
		(D)	20,000					4
(D)	20,000						20,000	5
							480,000	6
							(232,500)	7
							(72,000)	8
							(250,000)	9
						(100,000)		10
(EL)	40,000				(10,000)			11
(EL)	46,400				(11,600)			12
				(592,000)				13
				410,000				14
				82,000				15
(CY1)	16,000							16
		(CY2)	4,000		1,000			17
								18
	126,400		126,400					19
								20
				(100,000)				21
				4,000	(4,000)			22
				96,000		(96,000)		23
					(24,600)		(24,600)	24
						(196,000)	(196,000)	25
							0	26

Subsidiary Company S Income Distribution

Internally generated net income **(last six months)**	**$20,000**
Adjusted income	$ 20,000
NCI share	20%
NCI	**$ 4,000**

Parent Company P Income Distribution

Internally generated net income	$ 80,000
80% × Company S adjusted income of $20,000 **(last six months)**	16,000
Controlling interest	**$96,000**

Worksheet 3-8

Intraperiod Purchase; Subsidiary Books Not Closed on Purchase Date
Company P and Subsidiary Company S
Worksheet for Consolidated Financial Statements
For Year Ended December 31, 20X1

	(Credit balance amounts are in parentheses.)	Trial Balance	
		Company P	Company S
1	Current Assets	187,600	87,500
2	**Investment in Company S**	**118,400**	
3			
4			
5	Goodwill		
6	Equipment	400,000	80,000
7	Accumulated Depreciation	(200,000)	(32,500)
8	Liabilities	(60,000)	(12,000)
9	Common Stock, Company P	(250,000)	
10	Retained Earnings, **Jan. 1, 20X1, Company P**	(100,000)	
11	Common Stock, Company S		(50,000)
12	Retained Earnings, **Jan. 1, 20X1, Company S**		(45,000)
13	Sales	(500,000)	(182,000)
14	Cost of Goods Sold	350,000	120,000
15	Expenses	70,000	24,000
16	**Subsidiary Income**	**(16,000)**	
17	**Dividends Declared**		**10,000**
18			
19	**Purchased Income**		
20		0	0
21			
22	Consolidated Net Income		
23	To NCI (see distribution schedule)		
24	Balance to Controlling Interest (see distribution schedule)		
25	Total NCI		
26	Retained Earnings, Controlling Interest, Dec. 31, 20X1		
27			

Eliminations and Adjustments:

(CY1)   Eliminate the entries made in the investment account and in the subsidiary income account (same as Worksheet 3-7).
(CY2)   Eliminate intercompany dividends. Notice that Company P's share of the subsidiary dividends declared are from those declared *after* the purchase.
(EL)   Eliminate 80% of the subsidiary equity balances at the beginning of the year plus 80% of Company S's income earned as of July 1, 20X1, against the investment account. The share of preacquisition income is entered as *Purchased Income* to emphasize that this income was earned prior to the date of purchase by Company P. For elimination purposes, this account may be viewed as a supplement to retained earnings. Since the subsidiary also declared dividends *prior to July 1, 20X1*, the controlling percentage of those dividends should be eliminated in this entry by crediting Dividends Declared.
(D)   Distribute the $20,000 excess of cost over book value (same as Worksheet 3-7).

Worksheet 3-8 (see page 3-23)

Eliminations & Adjustments				Consolidated Income Statement	Minority Interest	Controlling Retained Earnings	Consolidated Balance Sheet	
Dr.		Cr.						
							275,100	1
(CY2)	4,000	(CY1)	16,000					2
		(EL)	86,400					3
		(D)	20,000					4
(D)	20,000						20,000	5
							480,000	6
							(232,500)	7
							(72,000)	8
							(250,000)	9
						(100,000)		10
(EL)	40,000				(10,000)			11
(EL)	36,000				(9,000)			12
				(682,000)				13
				470,000				14
				94,000				15
(CY1)	16,000							16
		(CY2)	4,000		2,000			17
		(EL)	**4,000**					18
(EL)	**14,400**			**14,400**				19
	130,400		130,400					20
								21
				(103,600)				22
				7,600	(7,600)			23
				96,000		(96,000)		24
					(24,600)		(24,600)	25
						(196,000)	(196,000)	26
							0	27

Subsidiary Company S Income Distribution

Internally generated net income	
entire year	**$38,000**
Adjusted income	$ 38,000
NCI share	20%
NCI	**$ 7,600**

Parent Company P Income Distribution

Internally generated net income	$ 80,000
80% × Company S adjusted income	
of $20,000 **(last six months)**	**16,000**
Controlling interest	**$96,000**

Worksheet 3-9

Vertical Format, Simple Equity Method
Paulos Company and Subsidiary Carlos Company
Worksheet for Consolidated Financial Statements
For Year Ended December 31, 20X2

Worksheet 3-9 (see page 3-27)

		Financial Statements		Eliminations & Adjustments			NCI	Consolidated Balance Sheet	
	Compare this worksheet to Worksheet 3-6. Note that eliminations and adjustments, explanations, as well as income distribution schedules are the same for Worksheet 3-9 as for Worksheet 3-6.	Paulos	Carlos	Dr.		Cr.			
1	**Income Statement:**								1
2	Sales	(400,000)	(300,000)					(700,000)	2
3	Cost of Goods Sold	200,000	120,000					320,000	3
4	Depreciation Expense—Building	40,000	15,000	(A4)	8,000			63,000	4
5	Depreciation Expense—Equipment	20,000	20,000			(A5)	3,200		36,800	5
6	Other Expenses	90,000	33,000	(A6)	2,000			125,000	6
7	Subsidiary Income	(80,000)		(CY1)	80,000				7
7a									7a
7b	Interest Expense		12,000	(A3)	2,650			14,650	7b
8	Net Income	(130,000)	(100,000)					(140,550)	8
9	Consolidated Net Income								9
10									10
11	NCI (see income distribution schedule)						(20,000)		11
12	Controlling Interest (see income distribution schedule)							(120,550)	12
13									13
14	**Retained Earnings Statement:**								14
15	Retained Earnings, Jan. 1, 20X2, Paulos	(728,000)		(D1)	4,000			(714,550)	15
16				(A3-6)	9,450				16
17									17
18									18
19									19
20	Retained Earnings, Jan. 1, 20X2, Carlos		(290,000)	(EL)	232,000		(58,000)		20
21	Net Income (carrydown)	(130,000)	(100,000)				(20,000)	(120,550)	21
22	Dividends Declared		20,000			(CY2)	16,000	4,000		22
23	Retained Earnings, Dec. 31, 20X2	(858,000)	(370,000)						23
24									24
25	Retained Earnings, NCI, Dec. 31, 20X2						(74,000)		25
26									26
27	Retained Earnings, Controlling Interest, Dec. 31, 20X2							(835,100)	27
28									28

Line	Account			Elim. Dr	Elim. Cr	NCI	Controlling R/E	Consolidated
29	**Balance Sheet:**							
30	Cash	312,000	160,000					472,000
31	Inventory	210,000	120,000					330,000
32	Land	200,000	150,000	(D2) 40,000				390,000
33	Building	800,000	600,000	(D4) 160,000				1,560,000
34	Accumulated Depreciation—Building	(120,000)	(330,000)		(A4) 16,000			(466,000)
35	Equipment	400,000	150,000		(D5) 16,000			534,000
36	Accumulated Depreciation—Equipment	(90,000)	(90,000)	(A5) 6,400				(173,600)
37	Investment in Carlos Company	796,000		(CY2) 16,000	(CY1) 80,000			
38					(EL) 432,000			
39					(D) 300,000			
40	Patent		100,000	(D6) 20,000	(A6) 4,000			116,000
40a	Goodwill			(D7) 81,400				81,400
41	Current Liabilities	(150,000)	(40,000)					(190,000)
42	Bonds Payable		(200,000)					(200,000)
43	Discount/Premium			(D3) 10,600	(A3) 5,300			5,300
44	Common Stock, Paulos	(1,500,000)						(1,500,000)
45	Common Stock, Carlos		(100,000)	(EL) 80,000		(20,000)		
46	Paid-In Capital in Excess of Par, Carlos		(150,000)	(EL) 120,000		(30,000)		
47	Retained Earnings, Dec. 31, 20X2 (carrydown)	(858,000)	(370,000)					
48	Retained Earnings, Controlling Interest, Dec. 31, 20X2						(835,100)	(835,100)
49								
50	Retained Earnings, NCI, Dec. 31, 20X2					(74,000)		
51	Total NCI					(124,000)		(124,000)
52	Total	0	0	872,500	872,500			0

Worksheet 3-10

Equity Method, Tax Issues
Paro Company and Subsidiary Sunstran Corporation
Worksheet for Consolidated Financial Statements
For Year Ended December 31, 20X1

	(Credit balance amounts are in parentheses.)	Trial Balance	
		Paro	Sunstran
1	Cash	324,000	30,000
2	Accounts Receivable (net)	354,000	95,000
3	Inventory	540,000	100,000
4	Land	100,000	30,000
5	Building	1,300,000	950,000
6	Accumulated Depreciation, Building	(400,000)	(300,000)
7	**Noncurrent Deferred Tax Expense**		
8	Investment in Sunstran Company	1,058,000	
9			
10			
11	Goodwill		
12	Current Liabilities	(248,000)	(20,000)
13	**Deferred Tax Liability**		
14			
15	Common Stock, Paro	(510,000)	
16	Retained Earnings, Jan. 1, 20X1, Paro	(1,950,000)	
17			
18	Common Stock, Sunstran		(100,000)
19	Paid-In Capital in Excess of Par, Sunstran		(300,000)
20	Retained Earnings, Jan. 1, 20X1, Sunstran		(400,000)
21			
22	Sales	(3,400,000)	(900,000)
23	Cost of Goods Sold	2,070,000	600,000
24	Expenses	530,000	150,000
25			
26	Subsidiary Income	(84,000)	
27	Provision for Tax	216,000	45,000
28			
29	Dividends Declared	100,000	20,000
30		0	0
31	Consolidated Net Income		
32	To NCI (see distribution schedule)		
33	Balance to Controlling Interest (see distribution schedule)		
34	Total NCI		
35	Retained Earnings, Controlling Interest, Dec. 31, 20X1		
36			

Worksheet 3-10 (see page 3-32)

Eliminations & Adjustments				Consolidated Income Statement	NCI	Controlling Retained Earnings	Consolidated Balance Sheet	
Dr.		Cr.						
							354,000	1
							449,000	2
							640,000	3
							130,000	4
							2,250,000	5
(D3)	160,000	(A3)	8,000				(548,000)	6
(D2)	60,000						60,000	7
(CY2)	16,000	(CY1)	84,000					8
		(EL)	640,000					9
		(D)	350,000					10
(D4)	220,000						220,000	11
							(268,000)	12
(A3t)	2,400	(D3t)	48,000				(111,600)	13
		(D4t)	66,000					14
							(510,000)	15
						(1,950,000)		16
								17
(EL)	80,000				(20,000)			18
(EL)	240,000				(60,000)			19
(EL)	320,000				(80,000)			20
								21
				(4,300,000)				22
				2,670,000				23
(A3)	8,000			688,000				24
								25
(CY1)	84,000							26
(D1)	24,000	(A3t)	2,400	282,600				27
								28
		(CY2)	16,000		4,000	100,000		29
	1,214,400		1,214,400					30
				(659,400)				31
				21,000	(21,000)			32
				638,400		(638,400)		33
					(177,000)		(177,000)	34
						(2,488,400)	(2,488,400)	35
							0	36

Eliminations and Adjustments:

(CY1)   Eliminate the parent's share of subsidiary income.
(CY2)   Eliminate the current year intercompany dividends. The investment account is adjusted now to its January 1, 20X2 balance so that it may be eliminated.
(EL)   Eliminate the 80% ownership portion of the subsidiary equity accounts against the investment. A $350,000 excess cost remains.
(D)   Distribute the $350,000 excess cost as follows, in accordance with the determination and distribution of excess schedule:
(D1)   Record the current portion of tax loss carryover used this period. It is assumed the parent reduced its provision for the carryover used.
(D2)   Record the noncurrent portion of the tax loss carryover.
(D3)   Increase the building by $160,000 by lowering accumulated depreciation.
(D3t) Record the deferred tax liability related to the building increase.
(D4)   Record the goodwill.
(D4t) Record the deferred tax liability applicable to goodwill.
(A3)   Record the annual increase in building depreciation; $160,000 net increase in the building divided by its 20-year life equals $8,000.
(A3t) Reduce the provision for tax account by 30% of the increase in depreciation expense ($2,400).

Subsidiary Sunstran Company Income Distribution

	Internally generated net income	$ 105,000
	Adjusted income	$ 105,000
	NCI share	20%
	NCI	**$ 21,000**

Parent Paro Company Income Distribution

Building depreciation . . . . (A3)	$ 8,000	Internally generated net income	$ 584,000
Current tax carryover . . . . **(D1)**	24,000	80% × Sunstran Company adjusted income of $105,000	84,000
		Decrease in provision for tax:	
		(A3t)	**2,400**
		Controlling interest	**$638,400**

Worksheet 4-1

Intercompany Sales; No Intercompany Goods in Inventories
Company P and Subsidiary Company S
Worksheet for Consolidated Financial Statements
For Year Ended December 31, **20X1**

	(Credit balance amounts are in parentheses.)	Trial Balance	
		Company P	Company S
1	**Accounts Receivable**	110,000	150,000
2	Inventory, Dec. 31, 20X1	70,000	40,000
3	Investment in Company S	196,000	
4			
5	Other Assets	314,000	155,000
6	**Accounts Payable**	(80,000)	(100,000)
7	Common Stock ($10 par), Company P	(200,000)	
8	Retained Earnings, Jan. 1, 20X1, Company P	(250,000)	
9	Common Stock ($10 par), Company S		(100,000)
10	Retained Earnings, Jan. 1, 20X1, Company S		(70,000)
11	**Sales**	(700,000)	(500,000)
12	**Cost of Goods Sold**	510,000	350,000
13	Expenses	90,000	75,000
14	Subsidiary Income	(60,000)	
15		0	0
16	Consolidated Net Income		
17	To NCI (see distribution schedule)		
18	Balance to Controlling Interest (see distribution schedule)		
19	Total NCI		
20	Retained Earnings, Controlling Interest, Dec. 31, 20X1		
21			

Eliminations and Adjustments:

(CY1) Eliminate the entry recording the parent's share of subsidiary net income.
(EL)   Eliminate against the investment in Company S account the pro rata portion of the subsidiary equity balances (80%) owned by the parent. To simplify the elimination, there is no discrepancy between the cost and book values of the investment in this example. Also, note that the worksheet process is expedited by always eliminating the intercompany investment first.
(IS)   Eliminate the intercompany sales to avoid double counting. Now only Company S's original purchase from third parties and Company P's final sale to third parties remain in the consolidated income statement.
(IA)   Eliminate the $25,000 intercompany trade balances resulting from the intercompany sale.

Worksheet 4-1 (see page 4-3)

Eliminations & Adjustments		Consolidated Income Statement	NCI	Controlling Retained Earnings	Consolidated Balance Sheet	
Dr.	Cr.					
	(IA) 25,000				235,000	1
					110,000	2
	(CY1) 60,000					3
	(EL) 136,000					4
					469,000	5
(IA) 25,000					(155,000)	6
					(200,000)	7
				(250,000)		8
(EL) 80,000			(20,000)			9
(EL) 56,000			(14,000)			10
(IS) 100,000		(1,100,000)				11
	(IS) 100,000	760,000				12
		165,000				13
(CY1) 60,000						14
321,000	321,000					15
		(175,000)				16
		15,000	(15,000)			17
		160,000		(160,000)		18
			(49,000)		(49,000)	19
				(410,000)	(410,000)	20
					0	21

Subsidiary Company S Income Distribution

Internally generated net income		$ 75,000
Adjusted income		$ 75,000
NCI share		20%
NCI		$ 15,000

Parent Company P Income Distribution

Internally generated net income		$100,000
80% × Company S adjusted income of $75,000		60,000
Controlling interest		$160,000

Worksheet 4-2

Intercompany Goods in Ending Inventory
Company P and Subsidiary Company S
Worksheet for Consolidated Financial Statements
For Year Ended December 31, **20X1**

	(Credit balance amounts are in parentheses.)	Trial Balance	
		Company P	Company S
1	Accounts Receivable	110,000	150,000
2	**Inventory, Dec. 31, 20X1**	**70,000**	**40,000**
3	Investment in Company S	196,000	
4			
5	Other Assets	314,000	155,000
6	Accounts Payable	(80,000)	(100,000)
7	Common Stock ($10 par), Company P	(200,000)	
8	Retained Earnings, Jan. 1, 20X1, Company P	(250,000)	
9	Common Stock ($10 par), Company S		(100,000)
10	Retained Earnings, Jan. 1, 20X1, Company S		(70,000)
11	Sales	(700,000)	(500,000)
12	**Cost of Goods Sold**	**510,000**	**350,000**
13	Expenses	90,000	75,000
14	Subsidiary Income	(60,000)	
15		0	0
16	Consolidated Net Income		
17	To NCI (see distribution schedule)		
18	Balance to Controlling Interest (see distribution schedule)		
19	Total NCI		
20	Retained Earnings, Controlling Interest, Dec. 31, 20X1		
21			

Eliminations and Adjustments:

(CY1)   Eliminate the entry recording the parent's share of subsidiary net income.
(EL)   Eliminate 80% of the subsidiary equity balances against the investment in Company S account. There is no excess of cost or book value in this example.
(IS)   Eliminate the intercompany sale.
(EI)   Eliminate the profit in the ending inventory.
(IA)   Eliminate the intercompany trade balances.

Worksheet 4-2 (see page 4-6)

Eliminations & Adjustments Dr.	Eliminations & Adjustments Cr.	Consolidated Income Statement	NCI	Controlling Retained Earnings	Consolidated Balance Sheet	
	(IA) 25,000				235,000	1
	(EI) 8,000				102,000	2
	(CY1) 60,000					3
	(EL) 136,000					4
					469,000	5
(IA) 25,000					(155,000)	6
					(200,000)	7
				(250,000)		8
(EL) 80,000			(20,000)			9
(EL) 56,000			(14,000)			10
(IS) 100,000		(1,100,000)				11
(EI) 8,000	(IS) 100,000	768,000				12
		165,000				13
(CY1) 60,000						14
329,000	329,000					15
		(167,000)				16
		13,400	(13,400)			17
		153,600		(153,600)		18
			(47,400)		(47,400)	19
				(403,600)	(403,600)	20
					0	21

Subsidiary Company S Income Distribution

Unrealized profit in ending inventory ....**(EI) $8,000**	Internally generated net income .... $ 75,000
	Adjusted income .... $ 67,000
	NCI share 20%
	NCI .... $ 13,400

Parent Company P Income Distribution

	Internally generated net income $100,000
	80% × Company S adjusted income of
	$67,000 53,600
	Controlling interest $153,600

Worksheet 4-3

Intercompany Goods in Beginning and Ending Inventories
Company P and Subsidiary Company S
Worksheet for Consolidated Financial Statements
For Year Ended December 31, **20X2**

	(Credit balance amounts are in parentheses.)	Trial Balance	
		Company P	Company S
1	Accounts Receivable	160,000	170,000
2	**Inventory, Dec. 31, 20X2**	**60,000**	**50,000**
3	Investment in Company S	244,000	
4			
5	Other Assets	354,000	165,000
6	Accounts Payable	(90,000)	(80,000)
7	Common Stock ($10 par), Company P	(200,000)	
8	**Retained Earnings, Jan. 1, 20X2, Company P**	**(410,000)**	
9	Common Stock ($10 par), Company S		(100,000)
10	**Retained Earnings, Jan. 1, 20X2, Company S**		**(145,000)**
11			
12	Sales	(800,000)	(600,000)
13	**Cost of Goods Sold**	**610,000**	**440,000**
14			
15	Expenses	120,000	100,000
16	Subsidiary Income	(48,000)	
17		0	0
18	Consolidated Net Income		
19	To NCI (see distribution schedule)		
20	Balance to Controlling Interest (see distribution schedule)		
21	Total NCI		
22	Retained Earnings, Controlling Interest, Dec. 31, 20X2		
23			

Eliminations and Adjustments:

(CY1)   Eliminate the entry recording the parent's share of subsidiary net income.

(EL)   Eliminate 80% of the subsidiary equity balances against the investment in Company S account. There is no excess of cost or book value in this example.

(BI)   Eliminate the intercompany profit of $8,000 (20% × $40,000) in the beginning inventory by reducing both the cost of goods sold and the beginning retained earnings accounts. 20% of the decrease in retained earnings is shared by the noncontrolling interest, since, in this case, the *selling company was the subsidiary*. If the parent had been the seller, only the controlling interest in retained earnings would be decreased. It should be noted that the $8,000 profit is shifted from 20X1 to 20X2, since, as a result of the entry, the 20X2 consolidated cost of goods sold balance is reduced by $8,000. This procedure emphasizes the concept that intercompany inventory profit is not eliminated but only deferred until inventory is sold to an outsider.

(IS)   Eliminate the intercompany sales to avoid double counting.

(EI)   Eliminate the intercompany profit of $6,000 (20% × $30,000) recorded by Company S for the intercompany goods contained in Company P's ending inventory, and increase the cost of goods sold balance by this same amount.

(IA)   Eliminate the intercompany trade balances.

Worksheet 4-3 (see page 4-7)

Eliminations & Adjustments		Consolidated Income Statement	NCI	Controlling Retained Earnings	Consolidated Balance Sheet	
Dr.	Cr.					
	(IA) 60,000				270,000	1
	(EI) 6,000				104,000	2
	(CY1) 48,000					3
	(EL) 196,000					4
					519,000	5
(IA) 60,000					(110,000)	6
					(200,000)	7
(BI) 6,400				(403,600)		8
(EL) 80,000			(20,000)			9
(EL) 116,000						10
(BI) 1,600			(27,400)			11
(IS) 120,000		(1,280,000)				12
(EI) 6,000	(BI) 8,000					13
	(IS) 120,000	928,000				14
		220,000				15
(CY1) 48,000						16
438,000	438,000					17
		(132,000)				18
		12,400	(12,400)			19
		119,600		(119,600)		20
			(59,800)		(59,800)	21
				(523,200)	(523,200)	22
					0	23

Subsidiary Company S Income Distribution

Unrealized profit in ending inventory, 20% × $30,000 ....(EI) $6,000	Internally generated net income	$ 60,000	
	Realized profit in beginning inventory, 20% × $40,000 ....(BI)	**8,000**	
	Adjusted income	$ 62,000	
	NCI share	20%	
	NCI	$ 12,400	

Parent Company P Income Distribution

Internally generated net income	$ 70,000
80% × Company S adjusted income of $62,000	49,600
Controlling interest	$119,600

Worksheet 4-4

Intercompany Goods in Beginning and Ending Inventories; Periodic Inventory
Company P and Subsidiary Company S
Worksheet for Consolidated Financial Statements
For Year Ended December 31, 20X2

	(Credit balance amounts are in parentheses.)	Trial Balance	
		Company P	Company S
1	Accounts Receivable	160,000	170,000
2	**Inventory, Jan. 1, 20X2**	**70,000**	**40,000**
3	Investment in Company S	244,000	
4			
5	Other Assets	354,000	165,000
6	Accounts Payable	(90,000)	(80,000)
7	Common Stock ($10 par), Company P	(200,000)	
8	**Retained Earnings, Jan. 1, 20X2, Company P**	**(410,000)**	
9	Common Stock ($10 par), Company S		(100,000)
10	**Retained Earnings, Jan. 1, 20X2, Company S**		**(145,000)**
11			
12	Sales	(800,000)	(600,000)
13	**Purchases**	**600,000**	**450,000**
14	**Inventory, Dec. 31, 20X2: Asset**	**60,000**	**50,000**
15	**Cost of Goods Sold**	**(60,000)**	**(50,000)**
16	Expenses	120,000	100,000
17	Subsidiary Income	(48,000)	
18		0	0
19	Consolidated Net Income		
20	To NCI (see distribution schedule)		
21	Balance to Controlling Interest (see distribution schedule)		
22	Total NCI		
23	Retained Earnings, Controlling Interest, Dec. 31, 20X2		
24			

Eliminations and Adjustments:

(CY1) Eliminate the entry recording the parent's share of subsidiary net income.

(EL) Eliminate 80% of the subsidiary equity balances against the investment in Company S account. There is no excess of cost or book value in this example.

(BI) Eliminate the intercompany profit of $8,000 (20% × $40,000) in the beginning inventory by reducing both the cost of goods sold and the beginning retained earnings accounts. 20% of the decrease in retained earnings is shared by the noncontrolling interest, since, in this case, the *selling company was the subsidiary*. If the parent had been the seller, only the controlling interest in retained earnings would be decreased. It should be noted that the $8,000 profit is shifted from 20X1 to 20X2, since, as a result of the entry, the 20X2 consolidated cost of goods sold balance is reduced by $8,000. This procedure emphasizes the concept that intercompany inventory profit is not eliminated but only deferred until inventory is sold to an outsider.

(IS) Eliminate the intercompany sales to avoid double counting.

(EI) Enter the combined ending inventories of Company P and Company S, $60,000 and $50,000, respectively, less the intercompany profit of $6,000 (20% × $30,000) recorded by Company S for the intercompany goods contained in Company P's ending inventory.

(IA) Eliminate the intercompany trade balances.

Worksheet 4-4 (see page 4-9)

Eliminations & Adjustments			Consolidated Income Statement	NCI	Controlling Retained Earnings	Consolidated Balance Sheet	
Dr.		Cr.					
	(IA)	60,000				270,000	1
	(BI)	**8,000**	102,000				2
	(CYI)	48,000					3
	(EL)	196,000					4
						519,000	5
(IA) 60,000						(110,000)	6
						(200,000)	7
(BI) 6,400					(403,600)		8
(EL) 80,000				(20,000)			9
(EL) 116,000							10
(BI) 1,600				(27,400)			11
(IS) 120,000			(1,280,000)				12
	(IS)	120,000	930,000				13
	(EI)	**6,000**				104,000	14
(EI) 6,000			(104,000)				15
			220,000				16
(CYI) 48,000							17
438,000		438,000					18
			(132,000)				19
			12,400	(12,400)			20
			119,600		(119,600)		21
				(59,800)		(59,800)	22
					(523,200)	(523,200)	23
						0	24

Subsidiary Company S Income Distribution

Unrealized profit in ending inventory, 20% × $30,000 .... (EI) **$6,000**	Internally generated net income	$ 60,000[a]	
	Realized profit in beginning inventory, 20% × $40,000 ...... (BI)	**8,000**	
	Adjusted income	$ 62,000	
	NCI share	20%	
	NCI	$ 12,400	

[a][$600,000 − ($40,000 + $450,000 − $50,000) − $100,000 = $60,000]

Parent Company P Income Distribution

	Internally generated net income	$ 70,000[b]
	80% × Company S adjusted income of $62,000	49,600
	Controlling interest	$119,600

[b][$800,000 − ($70,000 + $600,000 − $60,000) − $120,000 = $70,000]

Worksheet 4-5

Intercompany Sale of Depreciable Asset
Company P and Subsidiary Company S
Worksheet for Consolidated Financial Statements
For Year Ended December 31, **20X1**

	(Credit balance amounts are in parentheses.)	Trial Balance	
		Company P	Company S
1	Current Assets	15,000	20,000
2	**Machinery**	50,000	**(a) 230,000**
3	**Accumulated Depreciation—Machinery**	(25,000)	**(b) (100,000)**
4	Investment in Company S	120,000	
5			
6	Common Stock ($10 par), Company P	(100,000)	
7	Retained Earnings, Jan. 1, 20X1, Company P	(10,000)	
8	Common Stock ($10 par), Company S		(50,000)
9	Retained Earnings, Jan. 1, 20X1, Company S		(75,000)
10	Sales	(200,000)	(100,000)
11	Cost of Goods Sold	150,000	59,000
12	**Depreciation Expense**	30,000	**(b) 16,000**
13	**Gain on Sale of Machine**	**(10,000)**	
14	Subsidiary Income	(20,000)	
15		0	0
16	Consolidated Net Income		
17	To NCI (see distribution schedule)		
18	Balance to Controlling Interest (see distribution schedule)		
19	Total NCI		
20	Retained Earnings, Controlling Interest, Dec. 31, 20X1		
21			

Notes to Trial Balance:

(a) Includes machine purchased for $30,000 from Company P on January 1, 20X1.
(b) Includes $6,000 depreciation on machine purchased from Company P on January 1, 20X1.

Eliminations and Adjustments:

(CY1)   Eliminate the entry recording the parent's share of subsidiary net income for the current year.
(EL)   Eliminate 80% of the subsidiary equity balances against the investment account. There is no excess to be distributed.
(F1)   Eliminate the $10,000 gain on the intercompany sale of the machine, and reduce machine to book value.
(F2)   Reduce the depreciation expense and accumulated depreciation accounts to reflect the depreciation ($4,000 per year) based on the consolidated book value of the machine, rather than the depreciation ($6,000 per year) based on the sales price.

Worksheet 4-5 (see page 4-12)

Eliminations & Adjustments				Consolidated Income Statement		NCI		Controlling Retained Earnings	Consolidated Balance Sheet	
Dr.		Cr.								
									35,000	1
		(F1)	10,000						270,000	2
(F2)	2,000								(123,000)	3
		(CY1)	20,000							4
		(EL)	100,000							5
									(100,000)	6
								(10,000)		7
(EL)	40,000					(10,000)				8
(EL)	60,000					(15,000)				9
				(300,000)						10
				209,000						11
		(F2)	2,000	44,000						12
(F1)	10,000									13
(CY1)	20,000									14
	132,000		132,000							15
				(47,000)						16
				5,000		(5,000)				17
				42,000				(42,000)		18
						(30,000)			(30,000)	19
								(52,000)	(52,000)	20
									0	21

Subsidiary Company S Income Distribution

Internally generated net income	$25,000
Adjusted income	$25,000
NCI share	20%
NCI	$ 5,000

Parent Company P Income Distribution

Unrealized gain on sale				
of machine . . . .(F1) **$10,000**	Internally generated net income			
	(including sale of machine)	$30,000
	80% × Company S adjusted income of			
	$25,000	20,000
	Gain realized through use of			
	machine sold to subsidiary . . . .**(F2)**	**2,000**
	Controlling interest	$42,000

Worksheet 4-6

Intercompany Sale of Depreciable Asset
Company P and Subsidiary Company S
Worksheet for Consolidated Financial Statements
For Year Ended December 31, **20X2**

	(Credit balance amounts are in parentheses.)	Trial Balance	
		Company P	Company S
1	Current Assets	85,000	60,000
2	**Machinery**	50,000	(a) 230,000
3	**Accumulated Depreciation—Machinery**	(45,000)	(b) (116,000)
4			
5	Investment in Company S	139,200	
6			
7	Common Stock ($10 par), Company P	(100,000)	
8	**Retained Earnings, Jan. 1, 20X2, Company P**	(60,000)	
9	Common Stock ($10 par), Company S		(50,000)
10	Retained Earnings, Jan. 1, 20X2, Company S		(100,000)
11	Sales	(250,000)	(120,000)
12	**Cost of Goods Sold**	180,000	80,000
13	**Depreciation Expense**	20,000	(c) 16,000
14	Subsidiary Income	(19,200)	
15		0	0
16	Consolidated Net Income		
17	To NCI (see distribution schedule)		
18	Balance to Controlling Interest (see distribution schedule)		
19	Total NCI		
20	Retained Earnings, Controlling Interest, Dec. 31, 20X2		
21			

Notes to Trial Balance:

(a) Includes machine purchased for $30,000 from Company P on January 1, 20X1.
(b) Includes $12,000 accumulated depreciation ($6,000 per year) on machine purchased from Company P on January 1, 20X1.
(c) Includes $6,000 depreciation on machine purchased from Company P on January 1, 20X1.

Eliminations and Adjustments:

(CY1) Eliminate the entry recording the parent's share of subsidiary net income for the current year.
(EL)   Eliminate 80% of the subsidiary equity balances against the investment account. There is no excess to be distributed.
(F1)   Eliminate the gain on the intercompany sale as it is reflected in beginning retained earnings on the parent's trial balance. Since the sale was made by the *parent*, Company P, the entire unrealized gain at the beginning of the year (now $8,000) is removed from the controlling retained earnings beginning balance. If the sale had been made by the subsidiary, the adjustment of beginning retained earnings would be split 80% to the controlling interest and 20% to the noncontrolling interest.
(F2)   Reduce the depreciation expense and accumulated depreciation accounts to reflect the depreciation based on the consolidated book value of the asset on the date of sale. This entry will bring the accumulated depreciation account to its correct consolidated year-end balance.

Worksheet 4-6 (see page 4-13)

Eliminations & Adjustments				Consolidated Income Statement		NCI		Controlling Retained Earnings		Consolidated Balance Sheet		
Dr.		Cr.										
										145,000		1
		(F1)	10,000							270,000		2
(F1)	2,000									(157,000)		3
(F2)	2,000											4
		(CY1)	19,200									5
		(EL)	120,000									6
										(100,000)		7
(F1)	8,000							(52,000)				8
(EL)	40,000					(10,000)						9
(EL)	80,000					(20,000)						10
				(370,000)								11
				260,000								12
		(F2)	2,000	34,000								13
(CY1)	19,200											14
	151,200		151,200									15
				(76,000)								16
				4,800		(4,800)						17
				71,200				(71,200)				18
						(34,800)				(34,800)		19
								(123,200)		(123,200)		20
										0		21

Subsidiary Company S Income Distribution

Internally generated net income	$24,000
Adjusted income	$24,000
NCI share	20%
NCI	$ 4,800

Parent Company P Income Distribution

Internally generated net income	$50,000
80% of Company S adjusted income of $24,000	19,200
Gain realized through use of machine sold to subsidiary . . . . (F2)	**2,000**
Controlling interest	$71,200

Worksheet 4-7

Intercompany Sale of a Depreciable Asset; Subsequent Sale of Asset to an Outside Party
Company P and Subsidiary Company S
Worksheet for Consolidated Financial Statements
For Year Ended December 31, **20X2**

	(Credit balance amounts are in parentheses.)	Trial Balance	
		Company P	Company S
1	Current Assets	85,000	74,000
2	Machinery	50,000	200,000
3	Accumulated Depreciation—Machinery	(45,000)	(104,000)
4	Investment in Company S	136,000	
5			
6	Common Stock ($10 par), Company P	(100,000)	
7	**Retained Earnings, Jan. 1, 20X2, Company P**	**(60,000)**	
8	Common Stock ($10 par), Company S		(50,000)
9	Retained Earnings, Jan. 1, 20X2, Company S		(100,000)
10	Sales	(250,000)	(120,000)
11	Cost of Goods Sold	180,000	80,000
12	**Depreciation Expense**	20,000	**16,000**
13	**Loss on Sale of Machine**		**4,000**
14	Subsidiary Income	(16,000)	
15	**Gain on Sale of Machine**		
16		0	0
17	Consolidated Net Income		
18	To NCI (see distribution schedule)		
19	Balance to Controlling Interest (see distribution schedule)		
20	Total NCI		
21	Retained Earnings, Controlling Interest, Dec. 31, 20X2		
22			

Eliminations and Adjustments:

(CY1)   Eliminate the entry recording the parent's share of subsidiary net income for the current year.
(EL)   Eliminate 80% of the subsidiary equity balances against the investment account. There is no excess to be distributed.
(F3)   Eliminate the gain on the intercompany sale as it is reflected in the parent's beginning retained earnings account, adjust the current year's depreciation expense, and revise the recording of the sale of the equipment to an outside party to reflect the net book value of the asset to the consolidated company.

Worksheet 4-7 (see page 4-15)

Eliminations & Adjustments			Consolidated Income Statement	NCI	Controlling Retained Earnings	Consolidated Balance Sheet	
Dr.		Cr.					
						159,000	1
						250,000	2
						(149,000)	3
	(CY1)	16,000					4
	(EL)	120,000					5
						(100,000)	6
(F3) 8,000					(52,000)		7
(EL) 40,000				(10,000)			8
(EL) 80,000				(20,000)			9
			(370,000)				10
			260,000				11
	(F3)	2,000	34,000				12
	(F3)	4,000					13
(CY1) 16,000							14
	(F3)	2,000	(2,000)				15
144,000		144,000					16
			(78,000)				17
			4,000	(4,000)			18
			74,000		(74,000)		19
				(34,000)		(34,000)	20
					(126,000)	(126,000)	21
						0	22

Subsidiary Company S Income Distribution

Internally generated net income	$20,000
Adjusted income	$20,000
NCI share	20%
NCI	$ 4,000

Parent Company P Income Distribution

Internally generated net income	$50,000
80% × Company S adjusted income of $20,000	16,000
Gain realized on sale of machine . . . . (F3)	**8,000**[a]
Controlling interest	$74,000

[a]$10,000 original gain − $2,000 realized in 20X1

Worksheet 4-8

Intercompany Notes
Company P and Subsidiary Company S
Worksheet for Consolidated Financial Statements
For Year Ended December 31, **20X1**

	(Credit balance amounts are in parentheses.)	Trial Balance	
		Company P	Company S
1	Cash	35,000	20,400
2	**Note Receivable from Company S**	**10,000**	
3	**Interest Receivable**	**400**	
4	Property, Plant, and Equipment (net)	140,000	150,000
5	Investment in Company S	128,000	
6			
7	**Note Payable to Company P**		**(10,000)**
8	**Interest Payable**		**(400)**
9	Common Stock, Company P	(100,000)	
10	Retained Earnings, Jan. 1, 20X1, Company P	(200,000)	
11	Common Stock, Company S		(50,000)
12	Retained Earnings, Jan. 1, 20X1, Company S		(100,000)
13	Sales	(120,000)	(50,000)
14	**Interest Income**	**(400)**	
15	Subsidiary Income	(8,000)	
16	Cost of Goods Sold	75,000	20,000
17	Other Expenses	40,000	19,600
18	**Interest Expense**		**400**
19		0	0
20	Consolidated Net Income		
21	To NCI (see distribution schedule)		
22	Balance to Controlling Interest (see distribution schedule)		
23	Total NCI		
24	Retained Earnings, Controlling Interest, Dec. 31, 20X5		
25			

Eliminations and Adjustments:

(CY1) Eliminate the parent's share (80%) of subsidiary net income.

(EL) Eliminate the controlling portion (80%) of the Company S January 1, 20X1 stockholders' equity against the investment in Company S account. No excess results.

(LN1) Eliminate the intercompany note and accrued interest applicable to the note. This entry removes the *internal note* from the consolidated balance sheet.

(LN2) Eliminate the intercompany interest expense and revenue. Since an equal amount of expense and revenue is eliminated, there is no change in the combined net income as a result of this entry.

Worksheet 4-8 (see page 4-18)

Eliminations & Adjustments Dr.	Eliminations & Adjustments Cr.	Consolidated Income Statement	NCI	Controlling Retained Earnings	Consolidated Balance Sheet	
					55,400	1
	(LN1) 10,000					2
	(LN1) 400					3
					290,000	4
	(CY1) 8,000					5
	(EL) 120,000					6
(LN1) 10,000						7
(LN1) 400						8
					(100,000)	9
				(200,000)		10
(EL) 40,000			(10,000)			11
(EL) 80,000			(20,000)			12
		(170,000)				13
(LN2) 400						14
(CY1) 8,000						15
		95,000				16
		59,600				17
	(LN2) 400					18
138,800	138,800					19
		(15,400)				20
		2,000	(2,000)			21
		13,400		(13,400)		22
			(32,000)		(32,000)	23
				(213,400)	(213,400)	24
					0	25

Subsidiary Company S Income Distribution

	Internally generated net income	$10,000
	Adjusted income	$10,000
	NCI share	20%
	NCI	$ 2,000

Parent Company P Income Distribution

	Internally generated net income	$ 5,400
	80% × Company S adjusted income of $10,000	8,000
	Controlling interest	$13,400

Worksheet 4-9

Vertical Worksheet Alternative
Company P and Subsidiary Company S
Worksheet for Consolidated Financial Statements
For Year Ended December 31, **20X2**

Worksheet 4-9 (see page 4-23)

(Credit balance amounts are in parentheses.)	Trial Balance		Eliminations & Adjustments		NCI	Consolidated	
	Company P	Company S	Dr.	Cr.			
Income Statement							1
Sales	(600,000)	(530,000)	(IS) 150,000			(980,000)	2
Cost of goods sold	400,000	280,000	(EI) 10,000	(IS) 150,000		532,000	3
				(BI) 8,000			4
Depreciation expense	40,000	50,000		(F2) 1,000		89,000	5
Other expenses	60,000	70,000				130,000	6
Subsidiary income	(104,000)		(CY1) 104,000				7
Net income	(204,000)	(130,000)				(229,000)	8
NCI (see distribution schedule)					(25,600)		9
Controlling interest (see distribution schedule)						(203,400)	10
							11
Retained Earnings Statement							12
Retained earnings, Jan. 1, 20X2, Company P	(600,000)		(BI) 6,400			(589,100)	13
			(F1) 4,500				14
Retained earnings, Jan. 1, 20X2, Company S		(400,000)	(EL) 320,000				15
			(BI) 1,600				16
					(78,400)		17
Net income (carrydown)	(204,000)	(130,000)			(25,600)	(203,400)	18
Dividends declared		20,000		(CY2) 16,000	4,000		19
Retained earnings, Dec. 31, 20X2	(804,000)	(510,000)					20
NCI, retained earnings, Dec. 31, 20X2					(100,000)		21
Controlling interest, retained earnings, Dec. 31, 20X2						(792,500)	22
							23
Balance Sheet							24
Inventory	300,000	250,000		(EI) 10,000		540,000	25
Accounts receivable	120,000	180,000		(IA) 20,000		280,000	26
Plant assets	236,000	400,000		(F1) 5,000		631,000	27
Accumulated depreciation	(100,000)	(60,000)	(F1) 500			(158,500)	28
			(F2) 1,000				29
Investment in Company S	628,000		(CY2) 16,000	(CY1) 104,000			30
				(EL) 480,000			31
				(D) 60,000			32
Goodwill			(D) 60,000			60,000	33
Current liabilities	(80,000)	(60,000)	(IA) 20,000			(120,000)	34
Common stock, ($5 par), Company S		(200,000)	(EL) 160,000		(40,000)		35
Common stock, ($10 par), Company P	(300,000)					(300,000)	36
Retained earnings (carrydown)	(804,000)	(510,000)					37
Retained earnings, controlling interest, Dec. 31, 20X2						(792,500)	38
Retained earnings, NCI, Dec. 31, 20X2					(100,000)		39
Total NCI					(140,000)	(140,000)	40
Totals	0	0	854,000	854,000	0	0	41

Eliminations and Adjustments:

(CY1) Eliminate the current-year entries recording the parent's share (80%) of subsidiary net income.
(CY2) Eliminate intercompany dividends.
(EL) Eliminate the pro rata portion of the subsidiary equity balances owned by the parent (80%) against the balance of the investment account.
(D) Distribute the excess to the goodwill account according to the determination and distribution of excess schedule.
(IS) Eliminate the intercompany sales made during 20X2.
(BI) Eliminate the intercompany profit in the beginning inventory, 20% (0.25 ÷ 1.25) multiplied by $40,000. Since it was a subsidiary sale, the profit is shared 20% by the NCI.
(EI) Eliminate the intercompany profit (20%) applicable to the $50,000 of intercompany goods in the ending inventory.
(IA) Eliminate the intercompany trade balances.
(F1) Eliminate the intercompany gain remaining on January 1, 20X2, applicable to the sale of the machine by Company P ($5,000 original gain less one-half-year's gain of $500).
(F2) Reduce the depreciation expense and accumulated depreciation accounts ($1,000 for the current year) in order to reflect depreciation based on the original cost.

Subsidiary Company S Income Distribution

Unrealized profit in ending inventory (20% × $50,000) .... (EI) $10,000	Internally generated net income		$ 130,000
	Realized profit in beginning inventory (20% × $40,000) .... (BI)		8,000
	Adjusted income		$ 128,000
	NCI share		20%
	NCI		$ 25,600

Parent Company P Income Distribution

	Internally generated net income	$ 100,000
	Gain realized on sale of machine .... (F2)	1,000
	80% × Company S adjusted income of $128,000	102,400
	Controlling interest	$203,400

Worksheet 5-1

Intercompany Investment in Bonds, Year of Acquisition; Straight-Line Method of Amortization
Company P and Subsidiary Company S
Worksheet for Consolidated Balance Sheet
For Year Ended December 31, 20X3

	(Credit balance amounts are in parentheses.)	Trial Balance	
		Company P	Company S
1	Other Assets	56,400	220,000
2	**Interest Receivable**	**8,000**	
3	Investment in Company S Stock (90%)	100,800	
4			
5	**Investment in Company S Bonds (100%)**	**102,400**	
6	**Interest Payable**		**(8,000)**
7	**Bonds Payable, 8%**		**(100,000)**
8	Common Stock ($10 par), Company P	(100,000)	
9	Retained Earnings, Jan. 1, 20X3, Company P	(120,000)	
10	Common Stock ($10 par), Company S		(80,000)
11	Retained Earnings, Jan. 1, 20X3, Company S		(20,000)
12	Operating Revenue	(100,000)	(80,000)
13	Operating Expense	70,000	60,000
14	**Interest Income**	**(6,800)**	
15	**Interest Expense**		**8,000**
16	Subsidiary Income	(10,800)	
17	**Extraordinary Loss on Bond Retirement**		
18		0	0
19	Consolidated Net Income		
20	To NCI (see distribution schedule)		
21	Balance to Controlling Interest (see distribution schedule)		
22	Total NCI		
23	Retained Earnings, Controlling Interest, Dec. 31, 20X3		
24			

Eliminations and Adjustments:

(CY1)   Eliminate the entry recording the parent's share of subsidiary net income for the current year. This entry returns the investment in Company S stock account to its January 1, 20X3 balance to aid the elimination process.

(EL)   Eliminate 90% of the subsidiary equity balances of January 1, 20X3, against the investment in stock account. No excess results.

(B1)   Eliminate intercompany interest revenue and expense. Eliminate the balance of the investment in bonds against the bonds payable. Note that the investment in bonds is at its end-of-the-year amortized balance. The loss on retirement at the date the bonds were purchased is calculated as follows:

    Loss remaining at year-end:
        Investment in bonds at Dec. 31, 20X3 . . . . $102,400
        Less: Carrying value of bonds at Dec. 31, 20X3 . . . .   100,000 $2,400
    Loss amortized during year:
        Interest expense eliminated . . . . $ 8,000
        Less: Interest revenue eliminated   6,800   1,200
    Loss at Jan. 2, 20X3 . . . . $3,600

(B2)   Eliminate intercompany interest payable and receivable.

Worksheet 5-1 (see page 5-3)

Eliminations & Adjustments				Consolidated Income Statement	NCI	Controlling Retained Earnings	Consolidated Balance Sheet	
Dr.		Cr.						
							276,400	1
		(B2)	8,000					2
		(CY1)	10,800					3
		(EL)	90,000					4
		(B1)	102,400					5
(B2)	8,000							6
(B1)	100,000							7
							(100,000)	8
						(120,000)		9
(EL)	72,000				(8,000)			10
(EL)	18,000				(2,000)			11
				(180,000)				12
				130,000				13
(B1)	6,800							14
		(B1)	8,000					15
(CY1)	10,800							16
(B1)	3,600			3,600				17
	219,200		219,200					18
				(46,400)				19
				960	(960)			20
				45,440		(45,440)		21
					(10,960)		(10,960)	22
						(165,440)	(165,440)	23
							0	24

Subsidiary Company S Income Distribution

Extraordinary loss on		Internally generated net income,	
bond retirement . . . .(B1)	**$3,600**	**including interest expense**	**$12,000**
		Interest adjustment	
		($3,600 ÷ 3) . . . .(B1)	**1,200**
		Adjusted income	$ 9,600
		NCI share	10%
		NCI	$ 960

Parent Company P Income Distribution

Internally generated net income,	
including interest revenue	**$36,800**
90% × Company S adjusted income of	
$9,600	8,640
Controlling interest	$ 45,440

Worksheet 5-2

Intercompany Investment in Bonds, Year Subsequent to Acquisition; Straight-Line Method of Amortization
Company P and Subsidiary Company S
Worksheet for Consolidated Financial Statements
For Year Ended December 31, 20X4

	(Credit balance amounts are in parentheses.)	Trial Balance	
		Company P	Company S
1	Other Assets	94,400	242,000
2	Interest Receivable	8,000	
3	Investment in Company S Stock (90%)	120,600	
4			
5	**Investment in Company S Bonds (100%)**	101,200	
6	Interest Payable		(8,000)
7	Bonds Payable, 8%		(100,000)
8	Common Stock ($10 par), Company P	(100,000)	
9	**Retained Earnings, Jan. 1, 20X4, Company P**	(167,600)	
10	Common Stock ($10 par), Company S		(80,000)
11	**Retained Earnings, Jan. 1, 20X3, Company S**		(32,000)
12			
13	Operating Revenue	(130,000)	(100,000)
14	Operating Expense	100,000	70,000
15	Subsidiary Income	(19,800)	
16	Interest Expense		8,000
17	Interest Income	(6,800)	
18		0	0
19	Consolidated Net Income		
20	To NCI (see distribution schedule)		
21	Balance to Controlling Interest (see distribution schedule)		
22	Total NCI		
23	Retained Earnings, Controlling Interest, Dec. 31, 20X4		
24			

Eliminations and Adjustments:

(CY1)   Eliminate the entry recording the parent's share of subsidiary net income for the current year.
(EL)   Eliminate 90% of the subsidiary equity balances of January 1, 20X4, against the investment in stock account. There is no excess to be distributed.
(B1)   Eliminate intercompany interest revenue and expense. Eliminate the balance of the investment in bonds against the bonds payable. Note that the investment in bonds is at its end-of-the-year amortized balance. The remaining unamortized loss on retirement at the start of the year is calculated as follows:

> Loss remaining at year-end:
>   Investment in bonds at Dec. 31, 20X4 . . . . $101,200
>   Less: Carrying value of bonds at Dec. 31, 20X4 . . . .   100,000 $1,200
> Loss amortized during year:
>   Interest expense eliminated . . . . $ 8,000
>   Less: Interest revenue eliminated   6,800   1,200
>   Remaining loss at Jan. 1, 20X4 . . . . $2,400

The remaining unamortized loss of $2,400 on January 1, 20X4, is allocated 90% to the controlling retained earnings and 10% to the noncontrolling retained earnings since the bonds were issued by the subsidiary.
(B2)   Eliminate intercompany interest payable and receivable.

Worksheet 5-2 (see page 5-4)

Eliminations & Adjustments				Consolidated Income Statement	NCI	Controlling Retained Earnings	Consolidated Balance Sheet	
Dr.		Cr.						
							336,400	1
		(B2)	8,000					2
		(CY1)	19,800					3
		(EL)	100,800					4
		(B1)	**101,200**					5
(B2)	8,000							6
(B1)	**100,000**							7
							(100,000)	8
(B1)	**2,160**					(165,440)		9
(EL)	72,000				(8,000)			10
(EL)	28,800				(2,960)			11
(B1)	**240**							12
				(230,000)				13
				170,000				14
(CY1)	19,800							15
		(B1)	**8,000**					16
(B1)	**6,800**							17
	237,800		237,800					18
				(60,000)				19
				2,320	(2,320)			20
				57,680		(57,680)		21
						(13,280)	(13,280)	22
						(223,120)	(223,120)	23
							0	24

Subsidiary Company S Income Distribution

Internally generated net income, including interest expense		$22,000
Interest adjustment ($3,600 ÷ 3) . . . . **(B1)**		1,200
Adjusted income		$23,200
NCI share		10%
NCI		$ 2,320

Parent Company P Income Distribution

Internally generated net income, including interest revenue		$36,800
90% × Company S adjusted income of $23,200		20,880
Controlling interest		$57,680

Worksheet 5-3

Intercompany Bonds, Subsequent Period; Straight-Line Method of Amortization
Company P and Subsidiary Company S
Worksheet for Consolidated Financial Statements
For Year Ended December 31, 20X4

| | (Credit balance amounts are in parentheses.) | Trial Balance | |
		Company P	Company S
1	Other Assets	59,400	259,082
2	Investment in Company S Stock	143,874	
3			
4	Investment in Company S Bonds	101,800	
5	Bonds Payable		(100,000)
6	**Discount on Bonds**		**778**
7	Common Stock, Company P	(100,000)	
8	**Retained Earnings, Jan. 1, 20X4, Company P**	**(160,000)**	
9	Common Stock, Company S		(40,000)
10	**Retained Earnings, Jan. 1, 20X4, Company S**		**(110,000)**
11			
12	Sales	(80,000)	(50,000)
13	**Interest Income**	**(6,200)**	
14	Cost of Goods Sold	50,000	31,362
15	**Interest Expense**		**8,778**
16	Subsidiary Income	(8,874)	
17		0	0
18	Consolidated Net Income		
19	To NCI (see distribution schedule)		
20	Balance to Controlling Interest (see distribution schedule)		
21	Total NCI		
22	Retained Earnings, Controlling Interest, Dec. 31, 20X4		
23			

Eliminations and Adjustments:

(CY1)   Eliminate the entry recording the parent's share of subsidiary net income for the current year.

(EL)   Eliminate 90% of the January 1, 20X4, subsidiary equity balances against the January 1, 20X4, investment in Company S
stock balance. No excess results.

(B)   Eliminate intercompany interest revenue and expense. Eliminate the balance of the investment in bonds against the bonds
payable. Note that the investment in bonds and the discount on bonds are at their end-of-the-year amortized balances. The
remaining unamortized loss on retirement at the start of the year is calculated as follows:

Loss remaining at year-end:			
Investment in bonds at Dec. 31, 20X4		$101,800	
Less: Bonds payable at Dec. 31, 20X4	$100,000		
Discount on bonds at Dec. 31, 20X4	(778)	99,222	$2,578
Loss amortized during year:			
Interest expense eliminated		$ 8,778	
Less: Interest revenue eliminated		6,200	2,578
Remaining loss at Jan. 1, 20X4			$5,156

Since from the consolidated viewpoint the bonds were retired in the prior year and since the bonds were issued by the
subsidiary, the remaining unamortized loss of $5,156 on January 1, 20X4, is allocated 90% to the controlling retained
earnings and 10% to the noncontrolling retained earnings.

Worksheet 5-3 (see page 5-6)

Eliminations & Adjustments		Consolidated Income Statement	NCI	Controlling Retained Earnings	Consolidated Balance Sheet	
Dr.	Cr.					
					318,482	1
	(CY1) 8,874					2
	(EL) 135,000					3
	(B) 101,800					4
(B) 100,000						5
	(B) 778					6
					(100,000)	7
(B) 4,640				(155,360)		8
(EL) 36,000			(4,000)			9
(EL) 99,000			(10,484)			10
(B) 516						11
		(130,000)				12
(B) 6,200						13
		81,362				14
	(B) 8,778					15
(CY1) 8,874						16
255.230	255,230					17
		(48,638)				18
		1,244	(1,244)			19
		47,394		(47,394)		20
		(15,728)			(15,728)	21
				(202,754)	(202,754)	22
					0	23

Subsidiary Company S Income Distribution

Internally generated net income, including interest expense	$ 9,860
Interest adjustment	
($8,778 – $6,200) . . . . **(B)**	**2,578**
Adjusted income	$12,438
NCI share	10%
NCI	$ 1,244

Parent Company P Income Distribution

Internally generated net income, including interest revenue	$36,200
90% × Company S adjusted income of $12,438	11,194
Controlling interest	$47,394

Worksheet 5-4

Intercompany Bonds; Interest Method of Amortization
Company P and Subsidiary Company S
Worksheet for Consolidated Financial Statements
For Year Ended December 31, 20X4

	(Credit balance amounts are in parentheses.)	Trial Balance	
		Company P	Company S
1	Other Assets	59,333	259,082
2	Investment in Company S Stock	144,000	
3			
4	**Investment in Company S Bonds**	**101,887**	
5	**Bonds Payable**		**(100,000)**
6	**Discount on Bonds**		**918**
7	Common Stock, Company P	(100,000)	
8	Retained Earnings, Jan. 1, 20X4, Company P	(160,180)	
9	Common Stock, Company S		(40,000)
10	Retained Earnings, Jan. 1, 20X4, Company S		(110,200)
11			
12	Sales	(80,000)	(50,000)
13	**Interest Income**	**(6,220)**	
14	Cost of Goods Sold	50,000	31,358
15	**Interest Expense**		**8,842**
16			
17	Subsidiary Income	(8,820)	
18		0	0
19	Consolidated Net Income		
20	To NCI (see distribution schedule)		
21	Balance to Controlling Interest (see distribution schedule)		
22	Total NCI		
23	Retained Earnings, Controlling Interest, Dec. 31, 20X4		
24			

Eliminations and Adjustments:

(CY1)   Eliminate the entry recording the parent's share of subsidiary net income for the current year.
(EL)   Eliminate 90% of the January 1, 20X4, subsidiary equity balances against the January 1, 20X4, investment in Company S stock balance. No excess results.
(B)   Eliminate intercompany interest revenue and expense. Eliminate the balance of the investment in bonds against the bonds payable. Note that the investment in bonds and the discount on bonds are at their end-of-the-year amortized balances. The remaining unamortized loss on retirement at the start of the year is calculated as follows:

Loss remaining at year-end:			
Investment in bonds at Dec. 31, 20X4		$101,887	
Less: Bonds payable at Dec. 31, 20X4	$100,000		
Discount on bonds at Dec. 31, 20X4	(918)	99,082	$2,805
Loss amortized during year:			
Interest expense eliminated		$ 8,842	
Less: Interest revenue eliminated		6,220	2,622
Remaining loss at Jan. 1, 20X4			$5,427

Since from the consolidated viewpoint the bonds were retired in the prior year and since the bonds were issued by the subsidiary, the remaining unamortized loss of $5,427 on January 1, 20X4, is allocated 90% to the controlling retained earnings and 10% to the noncontrolling retained earnings.

Worksheet 5-4 (see page 5-8)

Eliminations & Adjustments			Consolidated Income Statement	NCI	Controlling Retained Earnings	Consolidated Balance Sheet	
Dr.		Cr.					
						318,415	1
	(CY1)	8,820					2
	(EL)	135,180					3
	(B)	**101,887**					4
(B)	**100,000**						5
	(B)	**918**					6
						(100,000)	7
(B)	**4,884**				(155,296)		8
(EL)	36,000			(4,000)			9
(EL)	99,180			(10,477)			10
(B)	**543**						11
			(130,000)				12
(B)	**6,220**						13
			81,358				14
	(B)	**8,842**					15
							16
(CY1)	8,820						17
	255,647	255,647					18
			(48,642)				19
			1,242	(1,242)			20
			47,400		(47,400)		21
			(15,719)			(15,719)	22
					(202,696)	(202,696)	23
						0	24

Subsidiary Company S Income Distribution

	Internally generated net income, including interest expense	$ 9,800
	Interest adjustment ($8,842 − $6,220) . . . .(B)	**2,622**
	Adjusted income	$12,422
	NCI share	10%
	NCI	$ 1,242

Parent Company P Income Distribution

	Internally generated net income, including interest revenue	$36,220
	90% × Company S adjusted income of $12,422	11,180
	Controlling interest	$47,400

Worksheet 5-5

Intercompany Capital Lease
Company P and Subsidiary Company S
Worksheet for Consolidated Financial Statements
For Year Ended December 31, 20X1

	(Credit balance amounts are in parentheses.)	Trial Balance	
		Company P	Company S
1	Accounts Receivable	30,149	44,793
2	**Minimum Lease Payments Receivable**	**4,000**	
3	**Unguaranteed Residual Value**	**1,000**	
4	**Unearned Interest Income**	**(533)**	
5	**Assets under Capital Lease**		**5,210**
6	**Accumulated Depreciation—Assets under Capital Lease**		**(1,737)**
7	Property, Plant, and Equipment	200,000	120,000
8	Accumulated Depreciation—Property, Plant, and Equipment	(80,000)	(50,000)
9	Investment in Company S	87,634	
10			
11	Accounts Payable	(21,000)	(5,000)
12	**Obligations under Capital Lease**		**(3,210)**
13	**Interest Payable**		**(514)**
14	Common Stock ($10 par), Company P	(50,000)	
15	Retained Earnings, Jan. 1, 20X1, Company S	(120,000)	
16	Common Stock ($5 par), Company S		(40,000)
17	Retained Earnings, Jan. 1, 20X1, Company S		(50,000)
18	Sales	(120,000)	(70,000)
19	**Interest Income**	**(616)**	
20	Subsidiary Income	(15,634)	
21	Operating Expense	65,000	38,207
22	**Interest Expense**		**514**
23	Depreciation Expense	20,000	11,737
24		0	0
25	Consolidated Net Income		
26	To NCI (see distribution schedule)		
27	Balance to Controlling Interest (see distribution schedule)		
28	Total NCI		
29	Retained Earnings, Controlling Interest, Dec. 31, 20X1		
30			

Worksheet 5-5 (see page 5-18)

Eliminations & Adjustments				Consolidated Income Statement	NCI	Controlling Retained Earnings	Consolidated Balance Sheet	
Dr.		Cr.						
							74,942	1
		(CL2)	4,000					2
		(CL2)	1,000					3
(CL2)	635	(CL1)	102					4
		(CL2)	5,210					5
(CL3)	1,737							6
(CL2)	5,851						325,851	7
		(CL3)	1,617				(131,617)	8
		(CY1)	15,634					9
		(EL)	72,000					10
							(26,000)	11
(CL2)	3,210							12
(CL2)	514							13
							(50,000)	14
						(120,000)		15
(EL)	32,000				(8,000)			16
(EL)	40,000				(10,000)			17
				(190,000)				18
(CL1)	616							19
(CY1)	15,634							20
				103,207				21
		(CL1)	514					22
		(CL3)	120	31,617				23
	100,197		100,197					24
				(55,176)				25
				3,908	(3,908)			26
				51,268		(51,268)		27
					(21,908)		(21,908)	28
						(171,268)	(171,268)	29
							0	30

Eliminations and Adjustments:

(CY1)   Eliminate the parent company's entry recording its share of Company S net income. This step returns the investment account to its January 1, 20X1, balance to aid the elimination process.

(EL)   Eliminate 80% of the January 1, 20X1, Company S equity balances against the investment in Company S balance.

(CL1) Eliminate the interest income recorded by the lessor, $616, and the interest expense recorded by the lessee, $514. The $102 disparity reflects the interest recorded on the unguaranteed residual value. This amount is returned to the unearned interest income.

(CL2) Eliminate the intercompany debt and the unguaranteed residual value. Eliminate the asset under capital lease and record the owned asset. The amounts are reconciled as follows:

Disparity in recorded debt:

Lessor balance, **$4,000 − $635** unearned interest income	$3,365
Lessee balance, **$3,210 + $514** accrued interest	3,724
Interest applicable to unguaranteed residual value	$ (359)
Unguaranteed residual value	**1,000**
Net original present value of unguaranteed residual value	$ 641
Asset under capital lease	**5,210**
Owned asset at original cost	$5,851

(CL3) Reclassify accumulated depreciation and adjust the depreciation expense to acknowledge cost of asset. The adjustment to depreciation expense is determined as follows:

Capitalized cost by lessee		$5,210
Depreciable cost:		
Cost	$5,851	
Less residual (salvage) value	1,000	4,851
Decrease in depreciable cost		$ 359
Adjustment to depreciation expense ($359 ÷ 3-year lease term)		**$ 120**

Subsidiary Company S Income Distribution

Internally generated net income, **including interest income on lease**	$19,542
Adjusted income	$19,542
NCI share	20%
NCI	$ 3,908

Parent Company P Income Distribution

Net interest eliminated (CL1)	**$102**	Internally generated net income, **including interest income on lease**	$35,616
		80% × Company S adjusted income of $19,542	15,634
		Decrease in depreciation (CL3)	**120**
		Controlling interest	$51,268

Worksheet 5-6

Intercompany Capital Lease, Subsequent Period
Company P and Subsidiary Company S
Worksheet for Consolidated Financial Statements
For Year Ended December 31, 20X2

	(Credit balance amounts are in parentheses.)	Trial Balance	
		Company P	Company S
1	Accounts Receivable	102,149	82,925
2	**Minimum Lease Payments Receivable**	**2,000**	
3	**Unguaranteed Residual Value**	**1,000**	
4	**Unearned Interest Income**	**(138)**	
5			
6	**Assets under Capital Lease**		**5,210**
7	**Accumulated Depreciation—Assets under Capital Lease**		**(3,474)**
8	Property, Plant, and Equipment	200,000	120,000
9	Accumulated Depreciation—Property, Plant, and Equipment	(100,000)	(60,000)
10	Investment in Company S	102,129	
11			
12	Accounts Payable	(41,000)	(15,000)
13	**Obligations under Capital Lease**		**(1,724)**
14	**Interest Payable**		**(276)**
15	Common Stock ($10 par), Company P	(50,000)	
16	**Retained Earnings, Jan. 1, 20X2, Company P**	**(171,250)**	
17	Common Stock ($5 par), Company S		(40,000)
18	Retained Earnings, Jan. 1, 20X2, Company S		(69,542)
19	Sales	(150,000)	(80,000)
20	**Interest Income**	**(395)**	
21	Subsidiary Income	(14,495)	
22	Operating Expense	100,000	49,868
23	**Interest Expense**		**276**
24	Depreciation Expense	20,000	11,737
25		0	0
26	Consolidated Net Income		
27	To NCI (see distribution schedule)		
28	Balance to Controlling Interest (see distribution schedule)		
29	Total NCI		
30	Retained Earnings, Controlling Interest, Dec. 31, 20X2		
31			

Worksheet 5-6 (see page 5-18)

Eliminations & Adjustments				Consolidated Income Statement	NCI	Controlling Retained Earnings	Consolidated Balance Sheet	
Dr.		Cr.						
							185,074	1
		(CL2)	2,000					2
		(CL2)	1,000					3
(CL2)	359	(CL1a)	119					4
		(CL1b)	102					5
		(CL2)	5,210					6
(CL3)	3,474							7
(CL2)	5,851						325,851	8
		(CL3)	3,234				(163,234)	9
		(CY1)	14,495					10
		(EL)	87,634					11
							(56,000)	12
(CL2)	1,724							13
(CL2)	276							14
							(50,000)	15
(CL1b)	102	(CL3)	120			(171,268)		16
(EL)	32,000				(8,000)			17
(EL)	55,634				(13,908)			18
				(230,000)				19
(CL1a)	395							20
(CY1)	14,495							21
				149,868				22
		(CL1)	276					23
		(CL3)	120	31,617				24
	114,310		114,310					25
				(48,515)				26
				3,624	(3,624)			27
				44,891		(44,891)		28
					(25,532)		(25,532)	29
						(216,159)	(216,159)	30
							0	31

Eliminations and Adjustments:

(CY1)   Eliminate the parent company's entry recording its share of Company S net income.
(EL)   Eliminate 80% of the January 1, 20X2, Company S equity balances against the investment in Company S balance.
(CL1a) Eliminate the interest income recorded by the lessor, $395, and the interest expense recorded by the lessee, $276. The $119 disparity reflects the interest recorded on the unguaranteed residual value. This amount is returned to the unearned interest income.
(CL1b) Adjust the unearned income and the parent's retained earnings for the $102 interest recorded in 20X1 on the unguaranteed residual value.
(CL2) Eliminate the intercompany debt and the unguaranteed residual value. Eliminate the asset under capital lease and record the owned asset. The amounts are reconciled as follows:

Disparity in recorded debt:

Lessor balance, **$2,000 − $359** unearned interest income	....	$1,641
Lessee balance, **$1,724 + $276** accrued interest	....	2,000
Interest applicable to unguaranteed residual value	....	$ (359)
Unguaranteed residual value	....	**1,000**
Net original present value of unguaranteed residual value	....	$ 641
Asset under capital lease	....	**5,210**
Owned asset at original cost	....	$5,851

(CL3) Reclassify accumulated depreciation. Adjust the depreciation expense for the current year and the controlling retained earnings for the preceding year to acknowledge cost of asset. The adjustment to the depreciation expense and the retained earnings is determined as follows:

Capitalized cost by lessee		$5,210
Depreciable cost:		
Cost	$5,851	
Less residual (salvage) value	1,000	4,851
Decrease in depreciable cost		$ 359
Adjustment to depreciation expense and retained earnings		
($359 ÷ 3-year lease term)		**$ 120**

Subsidiary Company S Income Distribution

	Internally generated net income, **including interest on lease**	$18,119
	Adjusted income	$18,119
	NCI share	20%
	NCI	$ 3,624

Parent Company P Income Distribution

Net interest eliminated .... (CL1a)		**$119**	Internally generated net income, **including interest income on lease**	$30,395
			80% × Company S adjusted income of $18,119	14,495
			Decrease in depreciation .... (CL3)	**120**
			Controlling interest	$44,891

Worksheet 6-1

Affiliates File Consolidated Income Tax Return
Company P and Subsidiary Company S
Worksheet for Consolidated Financial Statements
For Year Ended December 31, 20X3

	(Credit balance amounts are in parentheses.)	Trial Balance	
		Company P	Company S
1	Cash	205,000	380,000
2	Inventory	150,000	120,000
3	Investment in Company S	1,115,000	
4			
5			
6	Plant and Equipment	900,000	1,100,000
7	Accumulated Depreciation	(440,000)	(150,000)
8			
9	Patent		
10	Liabilities		(150,000)
11	Common Stock, Company S		(500,000)
12	Retained Earnings, 1/1/X3, Company S		(700,000)
13			
14	Common Stock, Company P	(800,000)	
15	Retained Earnings, 1/1/X3, Company P	(900,000)	
16			
17			
18	Sales	(600,000)	(400,000)
19	Cost of Goods Sold	350,000	200,000
20			
21	Depreciation Expense	25,000	20,000
22	Other Expenses	75,000	80,000
23	Patent Amortization Expense		
24	Subsidiary Income	(80,000)	
25	Total	0	0
26	**Consolidated Income Before Tax**		
27	**Consolidated Tax Provision**		
28	**Income Tax Payable**		
29	Consolidated Net Income		
30	NCI Share		
31	Controlling Share		
32	NCI		
33	Controlling Retained Earnings		
34	Total		

Worksheet 6–1 (see page 6-14)

Eliminations & Adjustments Dr.		Eliminations & Adjustments Cr.		Consolidated Income Statement	NCI	Controlling Retained Earnings	Consolidated Balance Sheet	
							585,000	1
		(EI)	35,000				235,000	2
		(CY1)	80,000					3
		(EL)	960,000					4
		(D)	75,000					5
(D)		(F1)	20,000				1,980,000	6
(F1)	4,000							7
(F2)	4,000						(582,000)	8
(D)	75,000	(A)	15,000				60,000	9
							(150,000)	10
(EL)	400,000				(100,000)			11
(EL)	560,000							12
(BI)	5,000				(135,000)			13
							(800,000)	14
(A)	10,000							15
(BI)	20,000							16
(F1)	16,000					(854,000)		17
(IS)	100,000			(900,000)				18
		(IS)	100,000					19
(EI)	35,000	(BI)	25,000	460,000				20
		(F2)	4,000	41,000				21
				155,000				22
(A)	5,000			5,000				23
(CY1)	80,000							24
	1,314,000		1,314,000					25
				(239,000)				26
(T)	71,700			71,700				27
		(T)	71,700				(71,700)	28
				(167,300)				29
				12,600	(12,600)			30
				154,700		(154,700)		31
					(247,600)		(247,600)	32
						(1,008,700)	(1,008,700)	33
	1,385,700		1,385,700				0	34

Eliminations and Adjustments:

(CY1) Eliminate the parent's entry recording its share of the current year's subsidiary income. This step returns the investment account to its balance on January 1, 20X3.

(EL) Eliminate 80% of the January 1, 20X3 subsidiary equity balances against the investment in Company S.

(D) Distribute the $75,000 excess of cost to the patent account.

(A) Amortize the patent at an annual amount of $5,000 for each of the past two years and for the current year.

(F1) Remove from retained earnings the undepreciated gain at the beginning of the year on the sale of the equipment. Since the sale was by the parent, the entire adjustment is removed from the controlling interest in retained earnings.

(F2) Adjust accumulated depreciation and the current year's depreciation expense for the $4,000 overstatement of depreciation caused by the original $20,000 intercompany gain.

(IS) Eliminate intercompany merchandise sales of $100,000 to avoid double counting.

(BI) Reduce the cost of goods sold by the $25,000 of intercompany profit included in the beginning inventory. Since the sale was made by the subsidiary, the reduction to retained earnings is borne 80% by the controlling interest and 20% by the NCI.

(EI) Reduce the ending inventory to its cost to the consolidated firm by decreasing it $35,000, and increase the cost of goods sold by $35,000.

(T) Record the provision for income tax, calculated as follows: $239,000 \times 0.3 = \$71,700$.

Subsidiary Company S Income Distribution

Gross profit on ending inventory (50% × $70,000) .... (EI)	$35,000	Internally generated net income before tax	$100,000
		Gross profit on beginning inventory (50% × $50,000) .... (BI)	25,000
		Adjusted income before tax	$ 90,000
		Company S share of taxes (30% × $90,000) .... **(T)**	**27,000**
		Company S net income	$ 63,000
		NCI share	20%
		NCI	$ 12,600

Parent Company P Income Distribution

Amortization of patent .... (A)	$ 5,000	Internally generated income before tax	$150,000
		Realized profit on equipment ($20,000 × 20%) .... (F2)	4,000
		Adjusted income before tax	$149,000
		Company P shares of taxes (30% × $149,000) .... **(T)**	**44,700**
		Company P net income	$104,300
		Share of subsidiary net income (80% × $63,000)	50,400
		Controlling interest	$154,700

Worksheet 6-2

Nonaffiliated Group for Tax Purposes
Company P and Subsidiary Company S
Worksheet for Consolidated Financial Statements
For Year Ended December 31, 20X4

	(Credit balance amounts are in parentheses.)	Trial Balance	
		Company P	Company S
1	Cash	19,200	80,000
2	Inventory, December 31, 20X4	170,000	150,000
3	Investment in Company S	504,000	
4			
5			
6	Plant and Equipment	600,000	550,000
7	Accumulated Depreciation	(410,000)	(120,000)
8			
9	Patent		
10	Current Tax Liability	(24,000)	(18,000)
11	**Deferred Tax Liability**	**(13,140)**	
12			
13	Common Stock, Company S		(250,000)
14	Retained Earnings, 1/1/X4, Company S		(350,000)
15			
16	Common Stock, Company P	(250,000)	
17	Retained Earnings, 1/1/X4, Company P	(510,450)	
18			
19			
20	Sales	(430,000)	(240,000)
21	Cost of Goods Sold	280,000	150,000
22			
23	Depreciation Expense	20,000	10,000
24	Other Expenses	50,000	20,000
25	Patent Amortization Expense		
26	**Provision for Tax**	**25,890**	**18,000**
27	Subsidiary Income	(31,500)	
28	Total	0	0
29	Consolidated Net Income		
30	NCI Share		
31	Controlling Share		
32	NCI		
33	Controlling Retained Earnings		
34	Total		

Worksheet 6–2 (see page 6-19)

Eliminations & Adjustments				Consolidated Income Statement	NCI	Controlling Retained Earnings	Consolidated Balance Sheet	
Dr.		Cr.						
							99,200	1
		(EI)	16,000				304,000	2
		(CY1)	31,500					3
		(EL)	450,000					4
		(D)	22,500					5
		(F1)	40,000				1,110,000	6
(F1)	8,000						(514,000)	7
(F2)	8,000							8
(D)	22,500	(A)	6,000				16,500	9
							(42,000)	10
(T1)	**19,158**	**(T2)**	**4,602**				1,416	11
								12
(EL)	187,500				(62,500)			13
(EL)	262,500	**(T1)**	**2,400**					14
(F1)	8,000				(81,900)			15
							(250,000)	16
(A)	4,500	**(T1)**	**16,758**					17
(BI)	24,000							18
(F1)	24,000					(474,708)		19
(IS)	100,000			(570,000)				20
(EI)	16,000	(IS)	100,000					21
		(BI)	24,000	322,000				22
		(F2)	8,000	22,000				23
				70,000				24
(A)	1,500			1,500				25
(T2)	**4,602**			48,492				26
(CY1)	31,500							27
	721,760		721,760					28
				(106,008)				29
				11,900	(11,900)			30
				94,108		(94,108)		31
					(156,300)		(156,300)	32
						(568,816)	(568,816)	33
							0	34

Eliminations and Adjustments:

(CY1)   Eliminate the parent's entry recording its share of subsidiary income for the current year. The entry now includes the parent's share of the subsidiary income after tax, since the companies are taxed as separate entities.

(EL)   Eliminate 75% of the January 1, 20X4 subsidiary equity balances against the investment in Company S.

(D)   Distribute the $22,500 excess of cost in the investment account to the patent account.

(A)   Amortize the patent for the current year and the three previous years at $1,500 per year.

(F1)   Eliminate the unamortized intercompany profit on the equipment sale by Company S as of January 1, 20X4. This elimination includes a $40,000 reduction in the asset account, an $8,000 decrease in accumulated depreciation, and a $32,000 (*before-tax*) decrease in beginning retained earnings. Since the sale was by the subsidiary, the retained earnings adjustment is allocated 75% to the controlling interest and 25% to the NCI.

(F2)   Adjust the current year's depreciation expense and accumulated depreciation by the $8,000 current year's portion of the inter-company profit on the equipment sale.

(IS)   Eliminate intercompany merchandise sales of $100,000 to avoid double counting.

(BI)   Remove the gross profit on intercompany sales recorded by Company P in 20X3 from its January 1, 20X4 retained earnings. The beginning inventory of Company S included $60,000 of goods sold by Company P with a gross profit of 40%, or $24,000. On a consolidated basis, the cost of goods sold is overstated, and this entry removes $24,000 from the consolidated cost of goods sold.

(EI)   Remove the $16,000 gross profit from the ending inventory and increase the cost of goods sold by the same amount. The Company S ending inventory includes $40,000 of goods sold by Company P with a gross profit of 40%.

(T1)   Adjust the beginning retained earnings balances and create a deferred tax asset (DTL) on prior-period adjustments as follows:

DTA/DTL adjustments:

To beginning retained earnings:

Subsidiary transactions:		Total Tax	Parent Share	Subsidiary Share
Beginning inventory	$ 0			
Remaining fixed asset profit	32,000			
Total	$32,000			
First tax (30% × $32,000)		$ 9,600	$ 7,200	$ 2,400
Second tax [20% × 30% × 75% × ($32,000 − $9,600 first tax)]		1,008	1,008	
Parent transactions:				
Beginning inventory	$24,000			
Remaining fixed asset profit	0			
Amortizations of excess	4,500			
Total	$28,500			
First tax (30% × $28,500)		8,550	8,550	
Total increase in retained earnings and DTA		**$19,158**	**$16,758**	**$2,400**

(T2) Adjust current-year tax provision and adjust deferred tax asset (DTA) for the tax effects of current-year income adjustments:

	Total Tax	Parent Share	Subsidiary Share
Subsidiary transactions:			
Beginning inventory	$ 0		
Ending inventory	0		
Fixed asset sale	0		
Realized fixed asset	(8,000)		
Total	$ (8,000)		
First tax (30% × $8,000)	$ (2,400)	$ (1,800)	$ (600)
Second tax [20% × 30% × 75% × ($8,000 − $2,400 first tax)]	(252)	(252)	
Parent transactions:			
Beginning inventory	$(24,000)		
Ending inventory	16,000		
Fixed asset sale	0		
Remaining fixed asset profit	0		
Amortizations of excess	1,500		
Total	$ (6,500)		
First tax (30% × $6,500)	(1,950)	(1,950)	
Increase (decrease) in DTA	**$(4,602)**	**$(4,002)**	**$(600)**

Subsidiary Company S Income Distribution

Internally generated income (before tax)	$ 60,000
Realized gain on fixed asset . . . . (F2)	8,000
Total income before tax	$ 68,000
Tax provision (30%)	(20,400)
Net income	$ 47,600
NCI share (25%)	**11,900**
Controlling share (75%)	$ 35,700

Parent Company P Income Distribution

Ending inventory profit . . . . (EI)	$16,000	Internally generated income (before tax)	$ 80,000
Patent amortization . . . . (A)	1,500	Realized beginning inventory profit . . . . (BI)	24,000
		Total income before tax	$ 86,500
		Tax provision (30%)	(25,950)
		Net income	$ 60,550
		Controlling share of subsidiary income (net of first tax)	35,700
		Second tax on share of subsidiary income (20% × 30% × $35,700)	(2,142)
		Total controlling interest	**$94,108**

Worksheet 7-1

Investment Acquired in Blocks; Immediate Control
Company P and Subsidiary Company S
Worksheet for Consolidated Financial Statements
For Year Ended December 31, 20X3

	(Credit balance amounts are in parentheses.)	Trial Balance	
		Company P	Company S
1	Current Assets	60,000	130,000
2	Investment in Company S	228,000	
3			
4			
5			
6	Building	400,000	80,000
7	Accumulated Depreciation—Building	(100,000)	(5,000)
8	Equipment		150,000
9			
10	**Accumulated Depreciation—Equipment**		(90,000)
11			
12	Goodwill		
13			
14	Liabilities	(100,000)	(30,000)
15	Common Stock, Company P	(200,000)	
16	**Retained Earnings, Jan. 1, 20X3, Company P**	**(210,000)**	
17			
18	Common Stock, Company S		(100,000)
19	Retained Earnings, Jan. 1, 20X3, Company S		(100,000)
20	Sales	(400,000)	(200,000)
21	Cost of Goods Sold	300,000	120,000
22	**Expenses**	**50,000**	**45,000**
23			
24	Subsidiary Income	(28,000)	
25		0	0
26	Consolidated Net Income		
27	To NCI (see distribution schedule)		
28	Balance to Controlling Interest (see distribution schedule)		
29	Total NCI		
30	Retained Earnings, Controlling Interest, Dec. 31, 20X3		
31			

Worksheet 7–1 (see page 7-4)

Eliminations & Adjustments		Consolidated Income Statement	NCI	Controlling Retained Earnings	Consolidated Balance Sheet	
Dr.	Cr.					
					190,000	1
	(CY) 28,000					2
	(EL) 160,000					3
	(D1) 30,000					4
	(D2) 10,000					5
					480,000	6
					(105,000)	7
(D1a) 18,000					172,800	8
(D2a) 4,800						9
	(A1a) 10,800				(102,400)	10
	(A2a) 1,600					11
(D1b) 12,000					17,200	12
(D2b) 5,200						13
					(130,000)	14
					(200,000)	15
(A1) 7,200				(202,800)		16
						17
(EL) 80,000			(20,000)			18
(EL) 80,000			(20,000)			19
		(600,000)				20
		420,000				21
(A1a) 3,600		100,200				22
(A2a) 1,600						23
(CY) 28,000						24
240,400	240,400					25
		(79,800)				26
		7,000	(7,000)			27
		72,800		(72,800)		28
			(47,000)		(47,000)	29
				(275,600)	(275,600)	30
					0	31

Eliminations and Adjustments:

(CY)   Eliminate the parent's entry recognizing 80% of the subsidiary net income for the current year. This entry restores the investment account to its balance at the beginning of the year, so that it can be eliminated against Company S beginning-of-the-year equity balances.

(EL)   Eliminate the 80% controlling interest in beginning-of-the-year subsidiary accounts against the investment account. The 60% and 20% investments could be eliminated separately if desired.

(D1)   The $30,000 excess of cost on the original 60% investment is distributed to the **(a)** equipment and **(b)** goodwill accounts according to the determination and distribution of excess schedule prepared on January 1, 20X1.

(A1a) Since the equipment has a 5-year remaining life on January 1, 20X1, the depreciation should be increased $3,600 per year for 3 years. This entry corrects the controlling retained earnings for the past 2 years by $7,200 and corrects the current depreciation expense by $3,600.

(D2)   The $10,000 excess of cost on the 20% block is distributed to the **(a)** equipment and **(b)** goodwill accounts according to the determination and distribution of excess schedule prepared on January 1, 20X3.

(A2a) The $4,800 excess attributable to the equipment is to be depreciated over 3 years. Therefore, current expenses are increased by $1,600.

Subsidiary Company S Income Distribution

Internally generated net income	$35,000
Adjusted income	$35,000
NCI share	20%
NCI	$ 7,000

Parent Company P Income Distribution

Equipment depreciation:			Internally generated net income	$50,000
Block 1, 60% . . . . **(A1a)**	$3,600		80% × Company S adjusted income of	
Block 2, 20% . . . . **(A2a)**	1,600		$35,000	28,000
			Controlling interest	$72,800

Worksheet 7-2

Investment Acquired in Blocks; Control Achieved with Second Block
Company P and Subsidiary Company S
Worksheet for Consolidated Financial Statements
For Year Ended December 31, 20X2

	(Credit balance amounts are in parentheses.)	Trial Balance	
		Company P	Company S
1	Current Assets	69,900	85,000
2	Investment in Company S	196,100	
3			
4			
5			
6	Building and Equipment	300,000	150,000
7			
8	**Accumulated Depreciation—Building and Equipment**	(200,000)	(30,000)
9			
10	**Goodwill**		
11	Liabilities		(20,000)
12	Common Stock, Company P	(100,000)	
13	**Retained Earnings, Jan. 1, 20X2, Company P**	(200,000)	
14	Common Stock, Company S		(50,000)
15	Retained Earnings, Jan. 1, 20X2, Company S		(115,000)
16	Sales	(300,000)	(100,000)
17	Cost of Goods Sold	200,000	60,000
18	**Expenses**	50,000	20,000
19			
20	Subsidiary Income	(16,000)	
21		0	0
22	Consolidated Net Income		
23	To NCI (see distribution schedule)		
24	Balance to Controlling Interest (see distribution schedule)		
25	Total NCI		
26	Retained Earnings, Controlling Interest, Dec. 31, 20X2		
27			

Eliminations and Adjustments:

(CY) Eliminate the parent's entry recognizing 80% of the subsidiary net income under the simple equity method. This entry restores the investment account to its balance at the beginning of the year.

(EL) Eliminate the 80% controlling interest in beginning-of-the-year subsidiary equity accounts against the investment account. If desired, the two investment blocks may be eliminated separately.

(D1) The remaining excess of cost over book value on the original 20% investment is $17,100 ($18,000 less 1 year of $900 amortization). It must be remembered that under the sophisticated equity method, amortization entries prior to securing control reduce the investment account. Always remember that only *the unamortized original excess remains*. The remaining $17,100 excess is carried to the building account according to the determination and distribution of excess schedule prepared on January 1, 20X1.

(A1) Building depreciation of $900 is recorded for the current year. Recall that no depreciation is needed for periods prior to achieving control, since that depreciation was recorded previously through the parent's investment account. Thus, the controlling retained earnings are already reduced.

(D2) The excess attributable to the January 1, 20X2 60% acquisition is distributed to the **(a)** building and equipment accumulated depreciation and **(b)** goodwill accounts according to the determination and distribution of excess schedule for this second acquisition.

(A2) Depreciation for the current year is increased $600 according to the January 1, 20X2 determination and distribution of excess schedule.

Worksheet 7–2 (see page 7-8)

Eliminations & Adjustments				Consolidated Income Statement	NCI	Controlling Retained Earnings	Consolidated Balance Sheet	
Dr.		Cr.						
							154,900	1
		(CY)	16,000					2
		(EL)	132,000					3
		(D1)	**17,100**					4
		(D2)	**31,000**					5
(D1)	**17,100**						472,500	6
(D2a)	**5,400**							7
		(A1)	900				(231,500)	8
		(A2a)	600					9
(D2b)	**25,600**						25,600	10
							(20,000)	11
							(100,000)	12
						(200,000)		13
(EL)	40,000				(10,000)			14
(EL)	92,000				(23,000)			15
				(400,000)				16
				260,000				17
(A1)	**900**			71,500				18
(A2a)	**600**							19
(CY)	16,000							20
	197,600		197,600					21
				(68,500)				22
				4,000	(4,000)			23
				64,500		(64,500)		24
					(37,000)		(37,000)	25
						(264,500)	(264,500)	26
							0	27

Subsidiary Company S Income Distribution

Internally generated net income	$20,000
Adjusted income	$20,000
NCI share	20%
NCI	$ 4,000

Parent Company P Income Distribution

Equipment depreciation:				
Block 1, 20%	**(A1)**	$900	Internally generated net income	$50,000
Block 2, 60%	**(A2a)**	600	80% × Company S adjusted income of $20,000	16,000
			Controlling interest	$64,500

Worksheet 7-3

Sale of Subsidiary Interest During Period; No Loss of Control
Company P and Subsidiary Company S
Worksheet for Consolidated Financial Statements
For Year Ended December 31, 20X3

	(Credit balance amounts are in parentheses.)	Trial Balance	
		Company P	Company S
1	Investment in Company S (60%)	244,500	
2			
3			
4	Equipment	600,000	100,000
5	Accumulated Depreciation—Equipment	(100,000)	(60,000)
6	Other Assets	581,500	305,000
7	Goodwill		
8	Common Stock, Company P	(500,000)	
9	Retained Earnings, Jan. 1, 20X3, Company P	(701,500)	
10			
11	Common Stock, Company S		(100,000)
12	Retained Earnings, Jan. 1, 20X3, Company S		(215,000)
13	Sales	(500,000)	(200,000)
14	Cost of Goods Sold	350,000	140,000
15	Expenses	50,000	30,000
16			
17	**Paid-In Capital in Excess of Par, Company P**	**(4,600)**	
18	Subsidiary Income	(19,900)	
19			
20	**Income Sold to NCI (second 20% block)**		
21		0	0
22			
23	Consolidated Net Income		
24	To NCI (see distribution schedule)		
25	Balance to Controlling Interest (see distribution schedule)		
26	Total NCI		
27	Retained Earnings, Controlling Interest, Dec. 31, 20X3		
28			

Worksheet 7–3 (see page 7-17)

Eliminations & Adjustments			Consolidated Income Statement	NCI	Controlling Retained Earnings	Consolidated Balance Sheet	
Dr.		Cr.					
	(CY)	18,000					1
	(EL)	189,000					2
	(D)	37,500					3
(D1) 15,000						715,000	4
	(A)	9,000				(169,000)	5
						886,500	6
(D2) 22,500						22,500	7
						(500,000)	8
(A) 6,000					(695,500)		9
							10
(EL) 60,000				(40,000)			11
(EL) 129,000				(86,000)			12
			(700,000)				13
			490,000				14
(NCI) 500			83,500				15
(A) 3,000							16
						(4,600)	17
(NCI) 1,900							18
(CY) 18,000							19
	(NCI)	2,400		(2,400)			20
255,900		255,900					21
							22
			(126,500)				23
			9,600	(9,600)			24
			116,900		(116,900)		25
			(138,000)			(138,000)	26
					(812,400)	(812,400)	27
						0	28

Eliminations and Adjustments:

(NCI) The income earned by the parent on the 20% interest sold on July 1, though earned by the controlling interest, now belongs to the NCI. The NCI owns 20% of the reported subsidiary income for the half-year ($12,000), which is $2,400. The NCI is unaffected by amortizations resulting from a previous price paid by the parent. Note that this entry credits the account, Income Sold to NCI, to accomplish the transfer of the income to the NCI. The offsetting debits are explained as follows:

20% of subsidiary income for the first six months, adjusted for one-fourth of the parent's
half-year amortization of excess or (20% $\times$ $12,000) − [$\frac{1}{4}$ $\times$ $\frac{1}{2}$ $\times$ $4,000] $1,900
Depreciation adjustment ($\frac{1}{4}$ $\times$ $\frac{1}{2}$ $\times$ $4,000)   500

Total debits $2,400

Amortization based on an 80% interest for the first half of the year is proper, since the consolidation involves an 80% controlling interest for the first half of the year and a 60% controlling interest for the second half of the year.

(CY) Eliminate the parent's entry recording its 60% share of subsidiary net income of $30,000. This entry restores the 60% interest to its simple-equity-adjusted cost at the beginning of the year so that the investment can be eliminated against subsidiary equity balances at the beginning of the year.

(EL) Eliminate 60% of the subsidiary equity balances at the beginning of the year against the investment account. An excess cost of $37,500 remains. This amount is three-fourths (60% ÷ 80%) of the original excess shown on page 7-11, since only a 60% interest is retained, as compared to an original investment of 80%.

(D) Since only three-fourths of the original investment remains, 75% of the excesses shown in the original determination and distribution of excess schedule on page 7-11 is recorded. Entry (D1) adjusts equipment and (D2) adjusts goodwill.

(A) 75% of the original $4,000 annual depreciation adjustments is recorded for the past two years and the current year. Note that the remaining depreciation adjustments applicable to the interest sold are already recorded.

Subsidiary Company S Income Distribution

Internally generated net income	$ 30,000
Adjusted income	$ 30,000
NCI share	40%
NCI for full year	$ 12,000
Less income purchased (20% × $12,000, first 6 months)	**2,400**
NCI	$ 9,600

Parent Company P Income Distribution

Depreciation adjustment on 60% interest . . . . . . (A)	$3,000	Internally generated net income	$100,000
		Adjusted income	$ 97,000
		60% × Company S adjusted income of $30,000	18,000
		20% × Company S adjusted income for first 6 months (net of amortization) . . .	**1,900**
		Controlling interest	$116,900

Worksheet 7-4

Subsidiary Preferred Stock, None Owned by Parent

Company P and Subsidiary Company S
Worksheet for Consolidated Financial Statements
For Year Ended December 31, 20X5

	(Credit balance amounts are in parentheses.)	Trial Balance	
		Company P	Company S
1	Current Assets	259,600	150,000
2	Property, Plant, and Equipment (net)	400,000	250,000
3	Investment in Company S Common Stock	195,600	
4			
5			
6	Goodwill		
7	Liabilities	(150,000)	(45,000)
8	Common Stock, Company P	(200,000)	
9	Retained Earnings, Jan. 1, 20X5, Company P	(340,000)	
10	Preferred Stock ($100 par), Company S		(100,000)
11	**Retained Earnings Allocated to Preferred Stock, Jan. 1, 20X5, Company S**		
12	Common Stock ($10 par), Company S		(100,000)
13	Retained Earnings, Jan. 1, 20X5, Company S		(130,000)
14			
15	Sales	(450,000)	(200,000)
16	Cost of Goods Sold	200,000	150,000
17	Expenses	100,000	25,000
18	Subsidiary Income	(15,200)	
19		0	0
20			
21	Consolidated Net Income		
22	To NCI (see distribution schedule)		
23	Balance to Controlling Interest (see distribution schedule)		
24	Total NCI		
25	Retained Earnings, Controlling Interest, Dec. 31, 20X5		
26			

Eliminations and Adjustments:

(PS) Distribute the beginning-of-the-period subsidiary retained earnings into the portions allocable to common and preferred stock. The typical procedure would be to consider the stated subsidiary retained earnings as applicable to common and to remove the preferred portion. This distribution reflects four years of arrearage (as of Jan. 1, 20X5) at $6,000 per year.

(CY) Eliminate the parent's entry recording its share of subsidiary current income.

(EL) Eliminate the pro rata subsidiary common stockholders' equity at the beginning of the period against the investment account. This entry includes elimination of the 80% of subsidiary retained earnings applicable to common stock.

(D) Distribute the excess of cost according to the determination and distribution of excess schedule.

Worksheet 7–4 (see page 7-21)

Eliminations & Adjustments		Consolidated Income Statement	NCI	Controlling Retained Earnings	Consolidated Balance Sheet	
Dr.	Cr.					
					409,600	1
					650,000	2
	(CY) 15,200					3
	(EL) 164,800					4
	(D) 15,600					5
(D) 15,600					15,600	6
					(195,000)	7
					(200,000)	8
				(340,000)		9
			(100,000)			10
	(PS) 24,000		(24,000)			11
(EL) 80,000			(20,000)			12
(PS) 24,000			(21,200)			13
(EL) 84,800						14
		(650,000)				15
		350,000				16
		125,000				17
(CY) 15,200						18
219,600	219,600					19
						20
		(175,000)				21
		9,800	(9,800)			22
		165,200		(165,200)		23
			(175,000)		(175,000)	24
				(505,200)	(505,200)	25
					0	26

Subsidiary Company S Income Distribution

Internally generated net income, (no adjustments)	$ 25,000
Less preferred cumulative claim to NCI . .	**(6,000)**
Common stock income	**$19,000**
NCI share	20%
NCI in common income	$ 3,800
Total NCI (**$6,000** + $3,800)	$ 9,800

Parent Company P Income Distribution

Internally generated net income	$150,000
80% × Company S adjusted income on common stock of $19,000	15,200
Controlling interest	$165,200

Worksheet 7-5

Subsidiary Preferred Stock Owned by Parent

Company P and Subsidiary Company S
Worksheet for Consolidated Financial Statements
For Year Ended December 31, 20X5

	(Credit balance amounts are in parentheses.)	Trial Balance	
		Company P	Company S
1	Current Assets	194,600	150,000
2	Property, Plant, and Equipment (net)	400,000	250,000
3	Investment in Company S Common Stock	195,600	
4			
5			
6	**Investment in Company S Preferred Stock**	75,800	
7			
8	Goodwill		
9	Liabilities	(150,000)	(45,000)
10	Common Stock, Company P	(200,000)	
11	**Paid-In Capital in Excess of Par, Company P**		
12	Retained Earnings, Jan. 1, 20X5, Company P	(347,200)	
13	Preferred Stock ($100 par), Company S		(100,000)
14	Retained Earnings Allocated to Preferred Stock, Jan. 1, 20X5, Company S		
15	Common Stock ($10 par), Company S		(100,000)
16	Retained Earnings, Jan. 1, 20X5, Company S		(130,000)
17			
18	Sales	(450,000)	(200,000)
19	Cost of Goods Sold	200,000	150,000
20	Expenses	100,000	25,000
21	Subsidiary Income—Common	(15,200)	
22	**Subsidiary Income—Preferred**	**(3,600)**	
23		0	0
24			
25	Consolidated Net Income		
26	To NCI (see distribution schedule)		
27	Balance to Controlling Interest (see distribution schedule)		
28	Total NCI		
29	Retained Earnings, Controlling Interest, Dec. 31, 20X5		
30			

Worksheet 7–5 (see page 7-23)

Eliminations & Adjustments		Consolidated Income Statement	NCI	Controlling Retained Earnings	Consolidated Balance Sheet	
Dr.	Cr.					
					344,600	1
					650,000	2
	(CY) 15,200					3
	(EL) 164,800					4
	(D) 15,600					5
	(CYP) 3,600					6
	(ELP) 72,200					7
(D) 15,600					15,600	8
					(195,000)	9
					(200,000)	10
	(ELP) 2,200				(2,200)	11
				(347,200)		12
(ELP) 60,000			(40,000)			13
(ELP) 14,400	(PS) 24,000		(9,600)			14
(EL) 80,000			(20,000)			15
(PS) 24,000			(21,200)			16
(EL) 84,800						17
		(650,000)				18
		350,000				19
		125,000				20
(CY) 15,200						21
(CYP) 3,600						22
297,600	297,600					23
						24
		(175,000)				25
		6,200	(6,200)			26
		168,800		(168,800)		27
			(97,000)		(97,000)	28
				(516,000)	(516,000)	29
					0	30

Eliminations and Adjustments:

(PS), (CY), (EL), and (D)	Same as Worksheet 7–4; the common stock investment elimination procedures are unaffected by the investment in preferred stock.
(CYP)	Eliminate the entry recording the parent's share of income allocable to preferred stock. If declared, intercompany preferred dividends would also have been eliminated. This adjustment restores the investment account to its beginning-of-the-period equity balance.
(ELP)	The parent's ownership portion of the par value and beginning-of-the-period retained earnings applicable to preferred stock is eliminated against the balance in the investment in preferred stock account. The difference in this case was an increase in equity, and it was carried to the controlling paid-in capital.

Subsidiary Company S Income Distribution

Internally generated net income (no adjustments)	$ 25,000
Less preferred cumulative claim:	
to NCI, 40% × $6,000	(2,400)
to controlling, 60% × $6,000	**(3,600)**
Common stock income	$ 19,000
NCI share	20%
NCI in common income	$ 3,800
Total NCI (**$2,400** + $3,800)	$ 6,200

Parent Company P Income Distribution

Internally generated net income	$150,000
60% × Company S income attributable to preferred stock	**3,600**
80% × Company S adjusted income on common stock of $19,000	15,200
Controlling interest	$168,800

Worksheet 7-6

Balance Sheet Only
Company P and Subsidiary Company S
Worksheet for Consolidated Balance Sheet
December 31, 20X4

	(Credit balance amounts are in parentheses.)	Trial Balance	
		Company P	Company S
1	Cash	61,936	106,535
2	Accounts Receivable	80,000	200,000
3	Inventory, Dec. 31, 20X4	60,000	150,000
4	Land	300,000	250,000
5	Building	800,000	600,000
6	Accumulated Depreciation—Building	(400,000)	(100,000)
7	Equipment	120,000	95,000
8	Accumulated Depreciation—Equipment	(70,000)	(30,000)
9	Investment in Company S Bonds	90,064	
10	Investment in Company S Stock	750,000	
11			
12	Goodwill		
13	Accounts Payable	(92,000)	(75,000)
14	Bonds Payable		(100,000)
15	Discount on Bonds Payable		3,465
16	Common Stock, Company P	(500,000)	
17	Retained Earnings, Dec. 31, 20X4, Company P	(1,200,000)	
18			
19			
20	Common Stock, Company S		(200,000)
21	Retained Earnings, Dec. 31, 20X4, Company S		(900,000)
22			
23		0	0
24	Total NCI		
25			

Eliminations and Adjustments:

(CV) Investment in Company S Stock is converted to the simple equity method as of *December 31, 20X4*, as follows: 80% × $300,000 increase in retained earnings = $240,000.

(EL) 80% of the subsidiary equity balances are eliminated against the investment in stock account.

(D) The $110,000 excess of cost is distributed according to the determination and distribution of excess schedule. Entry (D1) adjusts the building account and (D2) adjusts goodwill.

(A1) The excess attributable to the building is amortized for four years at $3,000 per year.

(IA) The intercompany trade balance is eliminated.

(EI) The gross profit of $16,000 (40% × $40,000) recorded by Company S and applicable to merchandise in Company P's ending inventory is deferred by reducing the inventory and retained earnings. Since the sale was made by Company S, the adjustment is allocated to the NCI and controlling retained earnings.

(F) As of December 31, 20X4, $2,000 (²⁄₅) of the profit on the equipment sale is still to be deferred. Since the sale was made by Company P, the controlling retained earnings absorb this adjustment, and the equipment and accumulated depreciation accounts are adjusted.

(B) Investment in Company S Bonds is eliminated against the net book value of the bonds. The net gain on the worksheet retirement is allocated to the NCI and controlling retained earnings, since the subsidiary originally issued the bonds.

Worksheet 7–6 (see page 7-27)

Eliminations & Adjustments					NCI	Consolidated Balance Sheet	
Dr.		Cr.					
						168,471	1
		(IA)	35,000			245,000	2
		(EI)	16,000			194,000	3
						550,000	4
						1,400,000	5
(D1)	30,000	(A)	12,000			(482,000)	6
		(F)	5,000			210,000	7
(F)	3,000					(97,000)	8
		(B)	90,064				9
(CV)	**240,000**	(EL)	880,000				10
		(D)	110,000				11
(D2)	80,000					80,000	12
(IA)	35,000					(132,000)	13
(B)	100,000						14
		(B)	3,465				15
						(500,000)	16
(A1)	12,000	**(CV)**	**240,000**			(1,418,377)	17
(EI)	12,800	(B)	5,177				18
(F)	2,000						19
(EL)	160,000				(40,000)		20
(EL)	720,000	(B)	1,294		(178,094)		21
(EI)	3,200						22
	1,398,000		1,398,000				23
					(218,094)	(218,094)	24
						0	25

Worksheet 8-1

Indirect Holdings; Intercompany Sales
Company A and Subsidiary Companies B and C
Worksheet for Consolidated Financial Statements
For Year Ended December 31, 20X3

	(Credit balance amounts are in parentheses.)	Trial Balance		
		Company A	Company B	Company C
1	Inventory, Dec. 31, 20X3	80,000	20,000	30,000
2				
3	Other Assets	60,000	146,000	130,000
4	Building and Equipment	300,000	200,000	150,000
5				
6	Accumulated Depreciation	(100,000)	(60,000)	(30,000)
7				
8	Investment in Company B	643,000		
9				
10				
11	Investment in Company C		318,000	
12				
13				
14	Common Stock ($10 par), Company A	(300,000)		
15	**Retained Earnings, Jan. 1, 20X3, Company A**	**(500,000)**		
16				
17				
18				
19	Common Stock ($10 par), Company B		(200,000)	
20	**Retained Earnings, Jan. 1, 20X3, Company B**		**(300,000)**	
21				
22				
23				
24	Common Stock ($10 par), Company C			(100,000)
25	**Retained Earnings, Jan. 1, 20X3, Company C**			**(150,000)**
26				
27	Sales	(400,000)	(300,000)	(150,000)
28	Cost of Goods Sold	250,000	160,000	80,000
29				
30				
31	Expenses	60,000	40,000	40,000
32				
33	Subsidiary or Investment Income	(93,000)	(24,000)	
34				
35		0	0	0
36	Consolidated Net Income			
37	To NCI, Company C (see distribution schedule)			
38	To NCI, Company B (see distribution schedule)			
39	To Controlling Interest (see distribution schedule)			
40	Total NCI			
41	Retained Earnings, Controlling Interest, Dec. 31, 20X3			
42				

Worksheet 8-1 (see page 8-16)

Eliminations & Adjustments				Consolidated Income Statement	NCI	Controlling Retained Earnings	Consolidated Balance Sheet	
Dr.		Cr.						
		(EIB)	2,500				124,500	1
		(EIC)	3,000					2
							336,000	3
(DB)	175,000						919,000	4
(DC)	94,000							5
		(AB)	52,500				(251,900)	6
		(AC)	9,400					7
		(CYB)	93,000					8
		(ELB)	375,000					9
		(DB)	175,000					10
		(CYC)	24,000					11
		(ELC)	200,000					12
		(DC)	94,000					13
							(300,000)	14
(AB)	35,000					(458,895)		15
(AC)	**3,525**							16
(BIB)	1,500							17
(BIC)	**1,080**							18
(ELB)	150,000				(50,000)			19
(ELB)	225,000				(72,965)			20
(AC)	**1,175**							21
(BIB)	500							22
(BIC)	**360**							23
(ELC)	80,000				(20,000)			24
(ELC)	120,000				(29,640)			25
(BIC)	**360**							26
(IS)	90,000			(760,000)				27
(EIB)	2,500	(IS)	90,000	401,700				28
(EIC)	3,000	(BIB)	2,000					29
		(BIC)	**1,800**					30
(AC)	**4,700**							31
(AB)	17,500			162,200				32
(CYB)	93,000							33
(CYC)	24,000							34
	1,122,200		1,122,200					35
				(196,100)				36
				5,760	(5,760)			37
				29,460	(29,460)			38
				160,880		(160,880)		39
					(207,825)		(207,825)	40
						(619,775)	(619,775)	41
							0	42

Eliminations and Adjustments:

(CYB) Eliminate the entry made by Company A to record its share of Company B income. This step returns the investment in the Company B account to its January 1, 20X3 balance to aid the elimination process.

(ELB) Eliminate 75% of the January 1, 20X3 Company B equity balances against the investment in Company B.

(DB)   Distribute the $175,000 excess of cost to the building and equipment account according to the determination and distribution of excess schedule applicable to the level one investment.

(AB)   Amortize the excess (added depreciation) according to the determination and distribution of excess schedule. This step requires adjustment of Company A retained earnings for 20X1 and 20X2, plus adjustment of 20X3 expenses.

(CYC) Eliminate the entry made by Company B to record its share of Company C income. This returns the investment in Company C account to its January 1, 20X3 balance to aid elimination.

(ELC) Eliminate 80% of the January 1, 20X3 Company C equity balances against the investment in Company C.

(DC)   Distribute the $94,000 excess of cost to the building and equipment account according to the determination and distribution of excess schedule applicable to the level two investment.

(AC)   Amortize the excess (added depreciation) according to the determination and distribution of excess schedule. Since it is created by actions of subsidiary Company B, the 20X2 amortization must be prorated 25% ($1,175) to the Company B NCI and 75% ($3,525) to the controlling interest. Note that the Company B NCI appears on the worksheet only after the first-level investment has been eliminated, again pointing to the need to eliminate the level one investment first.

(IS)   Eliminate intercompany sales to prevent double counting in the consolidated sales and cost of goods sold.

(BIB) Eliminate the Company B profit contained in the beginning inventory. Since Company B generated the sale, the correction of beginning retained earnings is split 75% to the controlling interest and 25% to the noncontrolling interest. The cost of goods sold is decreased since the beginning inventory was overstated.

(EIB) The cost of goods sold is adjusted and the ending inventory is reduced by the $2,500 of Company B profit contained in the ending inventory.

(BIC) Eliminate the Company C profit contained in the beginning inventory. Since Company C generated the retained earnings adjustment, it is apportioned as follows:

To NCI in Company C (20%)	$ 360
To NCI in Company B (25% of 80%)	360
To controlling interest (75% of 80%)	1,080
Total	$1,800

(EIC) The cost of goods sold is adjusted, and the ending inventory is reduced by the $3,000 of Company C profit contained in the ending inventory.

Company C Income Distribution

Ending inventory profit . . . . (EIC)	$ 3,000	Internally generated income	$ 30,000
		Beginning inventory profit . . . . **(BIC)**	**1,800**
		Adjusted income	$ 28,800
		Company B share, 80%	23,040
		Company C NCI, 20%	$ 5,760

Company B Income Distribution

Ending inventory profit . . . . (EIB)	$ 2,500	Internally generated income	$100,000
Building and equipment depreciation resulting from purchase of investment in Company C . . . . **(AC)**	**4,700**	Beginning inventory profit . . . . (BIB)	2,000
		80% of Company C adjusted income	23,040
		Adjusted income	$117,840
		Company A share, 75%	88,380
		Company B NCI, 25%	$ 29,460

Company A Income Distribution

Building and equipment depreciation resulting from investment in Company B . . . . (AB)	$17,500	Internally generated income	$ 90,000
		75% of Company B adjusted income	88,380
		Controlling interest	$160,880

Worksheet 8-2

Mutual Holdings, Treasury Stock Method
Company P and Subsidiary Company S
Worksheet for Consolidated Financial Statements
For Year Ended December 31, 20X3

	(Credit balance amounts are in parentheses.)	Trial Balance	
		Company P	Company S
1	Investment in Company S (80%)	248,000	
2			
3			
4	**Investment in Company P (10%), at cost**		**80,000**
5	Equipment	608,000	180,000
6	Accumulated Depreciation	(100,000)	(50,000)
7	Common Stock, Company P	(500,000)	
8	Retained Earnings, Jan. 1, 20X3, Company P	(200,000)	
9	Common Stock, Company S		(100,000)
10	Retained Earnings, Jan. 1, 20X3, Company S		(90,000)
11	Sales	(300,000)	(200,000)
12	Cost of Goods Sold	180,000	120,000
13	Expenses	80,000	60,000
14	Subsidiary Income	(16,000)	
15	**Treasury Stock (at cost)**		
16		0	0
17	Consolidated Net Income		
18	To NCI (see distribution schedule)		
19	Balance to Controlling Interest (see distribution schedule)		
20	Total NCI		
21	Retained Earnings, Controlling Interest, Dec. 31, 20X3		
22			

Eliminations and Adjustments:

(CY)   Eliminate the entry made by the parent during the current year to record its share of Company S income.
(EL)   Eliminate 80% of the January 1, 20X3 subsidiary equity balances against the investment in Company S account.
(D)   Distribute the excess of cost over book value to the equipment account as specified by the determination and distribution of excess schedule applicable to the level one investment.
(A)   Amortize the excess of $80,000 for the past two years and the current year.
(TS)   The investment in Company P must be at cost. If any equity adjustments have been made, they must be reversed and the investment in the parent returned to cost. If the shares are to be reissued, as is the case in this example, the investment is then transferred to the treasury stock account, a contra account to total consolidated stockholders' equity.

As an alternative to entry **(TS)**, the cost of the treasury shares could be used to retire them on the worksheet as follows:

Common Stock, Company P   50,000
Retained Earnings, Company P   30,000
   Investment in Company P   80,000

Worksheet 8-2 (see page 8-21)

Eliminations & Adjustments		Consolidated Income Statement	NCI	Controlling Retained Earnings	Consolidated Balance Sheet	
Dr.	Cr.					
	(CY) 16,000					1
	(EL) 152,000					2
	(D) 80,000					3
	(TS) 80,000					4
(D) 80,000					868,000	5
	(A) 12,000				(162,000)	6
					(500,000)	7
(A) 8,000				(192,000)		8
(EL) 80,000			(20,000)			9
(EL) 72,000			(18,000)			10
		(500,000)				11
		300,000				12
(A) 4,000		144,000				13
(CY) 16,000						14
(TS) 80,000					80,000	15
340,000	340,000					16
		(56,000)				17
		4,000	(4,000)			18
		52,000		(52,000)		19
			(42,000)		(42,000)	20
				(244,000)	(244,000)	21
					0	22

Subsidiary Company S Income Distribution

Internally generated net income	$20,000
Adjusted income	$20,000
NCI share	20%
NCI	$ 4,000

Parent Company P Income Distribution

Depreciation of excess for current year . . . . (A) $4,000	Internally generated net income	$40,000
	80% × Company S adjusted income of $20,000	16,000
	Controlling interest	$52,000

Worksheet 8-3

Mutual Holdings, Stock Swap
Company P and Subsidiary Company S
Worksheet for Consolidated Financial Statements
For Year Ended December 31, 20X3

	(Credit balance amounts are in parentheses.)	Trial Balance	
		Company P	Company S
1	Investment in Company S (80%)	248,000	
2			
3			
4			
5	**Investment in Company P (10%)**		**80,800**
6	Current Assets		80,000
7	Equipment	608,000	180,000
8	Accumulated Depreciation	(100,000)	(50,000)
9	Goodwill		
10	**Common Stock, Company P**	(500,000)	
11	**Retained Earnings, Jan. 1, 20X3, Company P**	(200,000)	
12	Common Stock, Company S		(130,000)
13	Paid-In Capital in Excess of Par, Company S		(50,000)
14	Retained Earnings, Jan. 1, 20X3, Company S		(90,000)
15	Sales	(300,000)	(200,000)
16	Cost of Goods Sold	180,000	120,000
17	Expenses	80,000	60,000
18	**Subsidiary (or Investment) Income**	(16,000)	**(800)**
19			
20		0	0
21	Consolidated Net Income		
22	To NCI		
23	Balance to Controlling Interest		
24	Total NCI		
25	Retained Earnings, Controlling Interest, Dec. 31, 20X3		
26			

Eliminations and Adjustments:

CYa Eliminate current year equity income recorded in Company P's Investment in Company S.
CYb Eliminate current year equity income recorded in Company S's Investment in Company P.
TR Transfer Investment in Company P to the parent's investment account.
EL Eliminate 11/13 of subsidiary equity against the Company S equity accounts.
D1 Distribute original $80,000 excess to equipment account.
D2 Distribute $3,539 excess on investment by Company S to goodwill.
A Amortize excess attributed to equipment for 2 prior and the current years.

Worksheet 8-3 (see page 8-23)

Eliminations & Adjustments		Consolidated Income Statement	NCI	Controlling Retained Earnings	Consolidated Balance Sheet	
Dr.	Cr.					
(TR) 80,800	(CYa) 16,000					1
	(CYb) 800					2
	(EL) 228,461					3
	(D) 83,539					4
	(TR) 80,800					5
					80,000	6
(D1) 80,000					868,000	7
	(A) 12,000				(162,000)	8
(D2) 3,539					3,539	9
					(500,000)	10
(A) 8,000				(192,000)		11
(EL) 110,000			(20,000)			12
(EL) 42,308			(7,692)			13
(EL) 76,153			(13,847)			14
		(500,000)				15
		300,000				16
(A) 4,000		144,000				17
(CYa) 16,000						18
(CYb) 800						19
421,600	421,600					20
		(56,000)				21
		4,000	(4,000)			22
		52,000		(52,000)		23
			(45,539)		(45,539)	24
				(244,000)	(244,000)	25
					0	26

Subsidiary Company S Income Distribution

Internally generated net income	$20,000
Adjusted income	$20,000
NCI share	20%
NCI	$ 4,000

Parent Company P Income Distribution

Depreciation of excess for current year . . . . (A) $4,000	Internally generated net income	$40,000
	80% × Company S adjusted income of	
	$20,000	16,000
	Controlling interest	$52,000

Worksheet 11-1

Consolidating the Foreign Subsidiary
Pome Corporation and Subsidiary Sori Corporation
Worksheet for Consolidated Financial Statements (in dollars)
For Year Ended December 31, 20X1

	(Credit balance amounts are in parentheses.) In U.S. dollars	Trial Balance	
		Pome Corporation	Sori Corporation
1	Cash	56,800	10,500
2	Accounts Receivable	112,000	22,050
3	Allowance for Doubtful Accounts	(5,600)	(1,050)
4	Due from Pome		14,700
5	Inventory, Dec. 31, 20X1	154,700	31,500
6	Prepaid Insurance	9,050	3,150
7	Investment in Sori Corporation	141,153	
8			
9			
10	Land	125,000	18,900
11	Depreciable Assets and Patents	500,000	126,000
12	Accumulated Depreciation and Amortization	(100,000)	(15,750)
13	Accounts Payable	(112,000)	(21,000)
14	Taxes Payable	(150,000)	(31,500)
15	Accrued Interest Payable	(16,000)	(1,050)
16	Mortgage Payable—Land	(105,000)	(10,500)
17	Common Stock	(350,000)	(80,000)
18	Paid-In Capital in Excess of Par	(100,000)	
19	Retained Earnings, Jan. 1, 20X1	(116,000)	(20,000)
20	**Cumulative Translation Adjustment—Sori**		(5,780)
21	**Cumulative Translation Adjustment—Pome**		
22			
23	Sales—Pome		(82,400)
24	Sales—Other	(908,600)	(206,000)
25	Gain on Sale of Depreciable Assets	(8,600)	(2,060)
26	Cost of Goods Sold	703,850	185,400
27	Depreciation and Amortization Expense	45,600	10,300
28	Income Tax Expense	108,000	30,900
29	Other Expenses (including interest)	51,800	23,690
30	Subsidiary Income	(36,153)	
31		0	0
32	Consolidated Net Income		
33	To Noncontrolling Interest		
34	Balance to Controlling Interest		
35	Total Noncontrolling Interest		
36	Retained Earnings, Controlling Interest, Dec. 31, 20X1		
37			

Worksheet 11-1 (see page 11-20)

Eliminations & Adjustments				Consolidated Income Statement	Minority Interest	Controlling Retained Earnings	Consolidated Balance Sheet	
Dr.		Cr.						
							67,300	1
							134,050	2
							(6,650)	3
		(IA)	14,700					4
							186,200	5
							12,200	6
		(CY1)	36,153					7
		(EL)	90,000					8
		(D)	**15,000**					9
							143,900	10
(D)	**15,750**						641,750	11
		(A)	**1,575**				(117,325)	12
(IA)	14,700						(118,300)	13
							(181,500)	14
							(17,050)	15
							(115,500)	16
(EL)	72,000				(8,000)		(350,000)	17
							(100,000)	18
(EL)	18,000				(2,000)	(116,000)		19
(CT)	**5,202**				(578)			20
		(CT)	5,202				(5,922)	21
(A)	**30**	**(D)**	**750**					22
(IS)	82,400							23
				(1,114,600)				24
				(10,660)				25
		(IS)	82,400	806,850				26
(A)	**1,545**			57,445				27
				138,900				28
				75,490				29
(CY1)	36,153							30
	245,780		245,780					31
				(46,575)				32
				4,017	(4,017)			33
				42,558		(42,558)		34
					(14,595)		(14,595)	35
						(158,558)	(158,558)	36
							0	37

Eliminations and Adjustments:

(CY1) Eliminate the entries in the subsidiary income account against the investment in Sori account to record the parent's 90% controlling interest in the subsidiary.

(EL) Eliminate 90% of the subsidiary's January 1, 20X1 equity balances against the balance of the investment account.

(CT) Distribute the cumulative translation adjustment between controlling interest and NCI.

(D) Distribute the excess of cost over book value of 15,000 FC to patent.

(A) Record appropriate patent amortization.

(IA) Eliminate the intercompany trade balances.

(IS) Eliminate the intercompany sales assuming that none of the goods purchased from Sori remain in Pome's ending inventory.

Subsidiary Sori Corporation Income Distribution

Internally generated net income	$40,170
Adjusted income	$40,170
Noncontrolling share	10%
NCI	$ 4,017

Parent Pome Corporation Income Distribution

Patent amortization (A)	$1,545	Internally generated net income	$ 7,950
		Share of subsidiary income (90% × $40,170) . . .	36,153
		Controlling interest	$42,558

Worksheet 11-2

Consolidating the Foreign Subsidiary
Pome Corporation and Subsidiary Sori Corporation
Worksheet for Consolidated Financial Statements (in dollars)
For Year Ended December 31, 20X1

	(Credit balance amounts are in parentheses.) In U.S. dollars	Trial Balance Pome Corporation	Sori Corporation
1	Cash	56,800	10,500
2	Accounts Receivable	112,000	22,050
3	Allowance for Doubtful Accounts	(5,600)	(1,050)
4	Due from Pome		14,700
5	Inventory, Dec. 31, 20X1	154,700	31,500
6	Prepaid Insurance	9,050	3,135
7	Investment in Sori Corporation	141,153	
8			
9			
10	Land	125,000	18,270
11	Depreciable Assets and Patents	500,000	122,400
12	Accumulated Depreciation and Amortization	(100,000)	(15,120)
13	Accounts Payable	(112,000)	(21,000)
14	Taxes Payable	(150,000)	(31,500)
15	Accrued Interest Payable	(16,000)	(1,050)
16	Mortgage Payable—Land	(105,000)	(10,500)
17	Common Stock	(350,000)	(80,000)
18	Paid-In Capital in Excess of Par	(100,000)	
19	Retained Earnings, Jan. 1, 20X1	(116,000)	(20,000)
20	**Remeasurement Gain**		(930)
21			
22			
23	Sales—Pome		(82,400)
24	Sales—Other	(908,600)	(206,000)
25	Gain on Sale of Depreciable Assets	(8,600)	(2,760)
26	Cost of Goods Sold	703,850	185,000
27	Depreciation and Amortization Expense	45,600	10,120
28	Income Tax Expense	108,000	30,900
29	Other Expenses (including interest)	51,800	23,735
30	Subsidiary Income	(36,153)	
31		0	0
32	Consolidated Net Income		
33	To Noncontrolling Interest		
34	Balance to Controlling Interest		
35	Total Noncontrolling Interest		
36	Retained Earnings, Controlling Interest, Dec. 31, 20X1		
37			

Worksheet 11-2 (see page 11-28)

Eliminations & Adjustments				Consolidated Income Statement	Minority Interest	Controlling Retained Earnings	Consolidated Balance Sheet	
Dr.		Cr.						
							67,300	1
							134,050	2
							(6,650)	3
		(IA)	14,700					4
							186,200	5
							12,185	6
		(CY1)	36,153					7
		(EL)	90,000					8
		(D)	15,000					9
							143,270	10
(D)	15,000						637,400	11
		(A)	1,500					12
(IA)	14,700						(118,300)	13
							(181,500)	14
							(17,050)	15
							(115,500)	16
(EL)	72,000				(8,000)		(350,000)	17
							(100,000)	18
(EL)	18,000				(2,000)	(116,000)		19
				(930)				20
								21
								22
(IS)	82,400							23
				(1,114,600)				24
				(11,360)				25
		(IS)	82,400	806,450				26
(A)	1,500			57,220				27
				138,900				28
				75,535				29
(CY1)	36,153							30
	239,753		239,753					31
				(48,785)				32
				4,141	(4,141)			33
				44,644		(44,644)		34
					(14,141)		(14,141)	35
						(160,644)	(160,644)	36
							0	37

Eliminations and Adjustments:

(CY1) Eliminate the entries in the subsidiary income account against the investment in the Sori account to record the parent's 90% controlling interest in the subsidiary.

(EL) Eliminate 90% of the subsidiary's January 1, 20X1 equity balances against the balance of the investment account.

(D) Distribute the excess of cost over book value of 15,000 FC.

(A) Record appropriate amortization of patent.
(IA) Eliminate the intercompany trade balances.
(IS) Eliminate the intercompany sales assuming that none of the goods purchased from Sori remain in Pome's ending inventory.

Subsidiary Sori Corporation Income Distribution

	Internally generated net income	$41,405*
	Adjusted income	$41,405
	Noncontrolling share	10%
	NCI	$ 4,141

Parent Pome Corporation Income Distribution

Patent amortization (A)	$1,500	Internally generated net income	$ 7,950
		Share of subsidiary income (90% × $41,405) .	37,264
		Remeasurement gain	**930**
		Controlling interest	$44,644

*This amount excludes the remeasurement gain of $930.

Worksheet SA1-1

Simple Equity Method, First Year
Paulos Company and Subsidiary Carlos Company
Worksheet for Consolidated Financial Statements
For Year Ended December 31, 20X1

		Trial Balance	
		Paulos	Carlos
1	Cash	100,000	50,000
2	Inventory	226,000	62,500
3	Land	200,000	150,000
4	Investment in Carlos Company	732,000	
5			
6			
7			
8	Buildings	800,000	600,000
9	Accumulated Depreciation	(80,000)	(315,000)
10	Equipment	400,000	150,000
11	Accumulated Depreciation	(50,000)	(70,000)
12	Patent (net)		112,500
13			
14	Goodwill		
15			
16	Current Liabilities	(100,000)	
17	Bonds Payable		(200,000)
18	Discount (premium)		
19			
20	Common Stock, Carlos		(100,000)
21	Paid-In Capital in Excess of Par, Carlos		(150,000)
22	Retained Earnings, Carlos		(250,000)
23	Common Stock, Paulos	(1,500,000)	
24	Retained Earnings, Paulos	(600,000)	
25	Sales	(350,000)	(200,000)
26	Cost of Goods Sold	150,000	80,000
27	Depreciation Exp.—Building	40,000	15,000
28	Depreciation Exp.—Equipment	20,000	20,000
29	Other Expenses	60,000	13,000
30	Interest Expense		12,000
31	Subsidiary Income	(48,000)	
32	Dividends Declared		20,000
33	Total	0	0
34	Consolidated Net Income		
35	NCI Share		
36	Controlling Share		
37	Total NCI		
38	Controlling Retained Earnings		
39	Total		

Worksheet SA1-1 (see page SA1-3)

Eliminations & Adjustments		Consolidated Net Income	NCI	Controlling Retained Earnings	Consolidated Balance Sheet	
Dr.	Cr.					
					150,000	1
					288,500	2
(D2) 50,000					400,000	3
	(CY1) 48,000					4
(CY2) 16,000						5
	(EL) 400,000					6
	(D) 300,000					7
(D4) 200,000					1,600,000	8
	(A4) 10,000				(405,000)	9
	(D5) 20,000				530,000	10
(A5) 4,000					(116,000)	11
(D6) 25,000						12
	(A6) 2,500				135,000	13
(D7) 101,750						14
					101,750	15
					(100,000)	16
					(200,000)	17
(D3) 13,248						18
	(A3) 3,312				9,936	19
(EL) 80,000			(20,000)			20
(EL) 120,000	(D) 74,998		(104,998)			21
(EL) 200,000			(50,000)			22
					(1,500,000)	23
				(600,000)		24
		(550,000)				25
(D1) 5,000		235,000				26
(A4) 10,000		65,000				27
	(A5) 4,000	36,000				28
(A6) 2,500		75,500				29
(A3) 3,312		15,312				30
(CY1) 48,000						31
	(CY2) 16,000		4,000			32
878,810	878,810					33
		(123,188)				34
		8,638	(8,638)			35
		114,550		(114,550)		36
		(179,636)			(179,636)	37
				(714,550)	(714,550)	38
					0	39

Eliminations and Adjustments:

(CY1)   Eliminate current year entries made to record subsidiary income.
(CY2)   Eliminate dividends paid by Carlos to Paulos. The investment is now at its January 1, 20X1
        balance.
(EL)   Eliminate 80% of subsidiary equity against the investment account.
(D)   Distribute $300,000 excess + $75,000 increase in NCI to:
(D1)   Cost of goods sold for inventory adjustment at time of purchase.
(D2)   Land adjustment.
(D3)   Record discount on bonds payable.
(D4)   Adjust building.
(D5)   Adjust equipment.
(D6)   Adjust patent.
(D7)   Record goodwill.

(A3–6) Account adjustments to be amortized:	Life	Annual Amount	Current Year	Prior Years	Total	Key
Bonds payable	4	3,312	3,312	0	3,312	A3
Buildings	20	10,000	10,000	0	10,000	A4
Equipment	5	(4,000)	(4,000)	0	(4,000)	A5
Patent (net)	10	2,500	2,500	0	2,500	A6
Total		11,812	11,812	0	11,812	

Income Distribution Schedules:

Subsidiary, Carlos

Amortizations of excess (Elim A) .... (A3–6)	$11,812	Internally generated net income	$ 60,000
Inventory adjustment .... (D1)	5,000		
		Adjusted income	$ 43,188
		NCI share	20%
		NCI	$ 8,638

Parent, Paulos

Internally generated net income	$ 80,000
80% Carlos adjusted income	34,550
Controlling interest	$114,550

Worksheet SA1-2

Simple Equity Method, First Year
Paulos Company and Subsidiary Carlos Company
Worksheet for Consolidated Financial Statements
For Year Ended December 31, 20X1

		Trial Balance	
		Paulos	Carlos
1	Cash	100,000	50,000
2	Inventory	226,000	62,500
3	Land	200,000	150,000
4	Investment in Carlos Company	732,000	
5			
6			
7			
8	Buildings	800,000	600,000
9	Accumulated Depreciation	(80,000)	(315,000)
10	Equipment	400,000	150,000
11	Accumulated Depreciation	(50,000)	(70,000)
12	Patent (net)		112,500
13			
14	Goodwill		
15			
16	Current Liabilities	(100,000)	
17	Bonds Payable		(200,000)
18	Discount (premium)		
19			
20	Common Stock, Carlos		(100,000)
21	Paid-In Capital in Excess of Par, Carlos		(150,000)
22	Retained Earnings, Carlos		(250,000)
23	Common Stock, Paulos	(1,500,000)	
24	Retained Earnings, Paulos	(600,000)	
25	Sales	(350,000)	(200,000)
26	Cost of Goods Sold	150,000	80,000
27	Depreciation Exp.—Building	40,000	15,000
28	Depreciation Exp.—Equipment	20,000	20,000
29	Other Expenses	60,000	13,000
30	Interest Expense		12,000
31	Subsidiary Income	(48,000)	
32	Dividends Declared		20,000
33	Total	0	0
34	Consolidated Net Income		
35	NCI Share		
36	Controlling Share		
37	Total NCI		
38	Controlling Retained Earnings		
39	Total		

Worksheet SA1-2 (see page SA1-6)

Eliminations & Adjustments				Consolidated Net Income	NCI	Controlling Retained Earnings	Consolidated Balance Sheet	
Dr.		Cr.						
							150,000	1
							288,500	2
(D2)	50,000						400,000	3
		(CY1)	48,000					4
(CY2)	16,000							5
		(EL)	400,000					6
		(D)	300,000					7
(D4)	200,000						1,600,000	8
		(A4)	10,000				(405,000)	9
		(D5)	20,000				530,000	10
(A5)	4,000						(116,000)	11
(D6)	25,000							12
		(A6)	2,500				135,000	13
(D7)	81,400							14
							81,400	15
							(100,000)	16
							(200,000)	17
								18
(D3)	13,248						9,936	19
		(A3)	3,312					20
(EL)	80,000				(20,000)			21
(EL)	120,000	(D)	54,648		(84,648)			22
(EL)	200,000				(50,000)			23
							(1,500,000)	24
						(600,000)		25
				(550,000)				26
(D1)	5,000			235,000				27
(A4)	10,000			65,000				28
		(A5)	4,000	36,000				29
(A6)	2,500			75,500				30
(A3)	3,312			15,312				31
(CY1)	48,000							32
		(CY2)	16,000		4,000			33
	858,460		858,460					34
				(123,188)				35
				8,638	(8,638)			36
				114,550		(114,550)		37
					(159,286)		(159,286)	38
						(714,550)	(714,550)	39
							0	

Eliminations and Adjustments:

(CY1) Eliminate current year entries made to record subsidiary income.
(CY2) Eliminate dividends paid by Carlos to Paulos. The investment is now at its January 1, 20X1 balance.
(EL)   Eliminate 80% of subsidiary equity against the investment account.
(D)   Distribute $300,000 excess + $54,650 increase in NCI to:
(D1)   Cost of goods sold for inventory adjustment at time of purchase.
(D2)   Land adjustment.
(D3)   Record discount on bonds payable.
(D4)   Adjust building.
(D5)   Adjust equipment.
(D6)   Adjust patent.
(D7)   Record goodwill.

(A3–6)	Account adjustments to be amortized:	Life	Annual Amount	Current Year	Prior Years	Total	Key
	Bonds payable	4	3,312	3,312	0	3,312	A3
	Buildings	20	10,000	10,000	0	10,000	A4
	Equipment	5	(4,000)	(4,000)	0	(4,000)	A5
	Patent (net)	10	2,500	2,500	0	2,500	A6
	Total		11,812	11,812	0	11,812	

Income Distribution Schedules:

Subsidiary, Carlos

Amortizations of excess (Elim. A) . . . . (A3–6)	$11,812	Internally generated net income	$ 60,000
Inventory adjustment . . . . (D1)	5,000		
		Adjusted income	$ 43,188
		NCI share	20%
		NCI	$ 8,638

Parent, Paulos

	Internally generated net income	$ 80,000
	80% Carlos adjusted income	34,550
	Controlling interest	$114,550

CITY OF MILWAUKEE
COMBINED FINANCIAL STATEMENTS
FOR THE YEAR ENDED DECEMBER 31, 1999

Source: City of Milwaukee Web site. For the full report, go to http://www.ci.mil.wi.us/citygov/comptrol/
comphome.htm

CITY OF MILWAUKEE
COMBINED BALANCE SHEET -
ALL FUND TYPES, ACCOUNT GROUPS AND DISCRETELY PRESENTED COMPONENT UNITS
DECEMBER 31, 1999
WITH COMPARATIVE TOTALS FOR DECEMBER 31, 1998
(Thousands of Dollars)

Exhibit 1

| | Governmental Fund Types | | | |
	General	Special Revenue	Debt Service	Capital Projects
ASSETS AND OTHER DEBITS				
Assets:				
Cash and cash equivalents	$ 34,662	$ 14,532	$ 40,205	$ 24,976
Investments			65,630	
Receivables (net):				
Taxes	21,280	7,716		
Accounts	9,376	2,351		
Unbilled accounts	1,170			519
Special assessments				13,583
Notes and loans	931	6,385	20,169	
Accrued interest	564		425	
Due from other funds	14,092		1,036	12
Due from primary government				
Due from component units	3,251		10,500	
Due from other governmental agencies		9,853		3,547
Advances to other funds	13,253			
Inventory of materials and supplies	6,428			213
Inventory of property for resale	26			
Prepaid items	721			
Other assets				
Restricted Assets:				
Cash and cash equivalents				
Investments	281			
Loans receivables				
Land				
Buildings				
Improvements other than buildings				
Machinery and equipment				
Furniture and furnishings				
Construction work in progress				
Nonutility property				
Accumulated depreciation				
Other Debits:				
Resources available in Governmental Funds				
Resources to be Provided for:				
Retirement of general obligation debt				
Pension contribution payable from subsequent year's budget				
Unfunded compensated absences				
Unfunded claims and judgments				
Total Assets and Other Debits	**$ 106,035**	**$ 40,837**	**$ 137,965**	**$ 42,850**
LIABILITIES, FUND EQUITY AND OTHER CREDITS				
Liabilities:				
Accounts payable	$ 14,606	$ 5,363	$	$ 6,483
Accrued wages	25,180	253		273
Accrued expenses				

Exhibit 1 (Continued)

Enterprise	Internal Service	Trust and Agency	General Fixed Assets	General Long-Term Obligations	Totals (Memorandum Only) Primary Government	Component Units	1999	1998 (Restated)
$ 20,085	$	$ 242,032	$	$	$ 376,492	$ 42,452	$ 418,944	$ 446,416
		1,130			66,760	11,815	78,575	94,515
		98,396			127,392		127,392	129,981
20,162		56			32,464	2,103	34,567	28,834
9,620					10,790		10,790	8,933
					13,583		13,583	12,424
		485			27,970	48,614	76,584	82,936
					989	436	1,425	2,457
456					15,596	1,738	17,334	32,904
					-	18	18	377
					13,751		13,751	15,971
					13,400	10,107	23,507	21,544
					13,253		13,253	10,979
2,705					9,346	541	9,887	9,346
					26	13,565	13,591	9,102
125					846	1,583	2,429	3,280
1,511					1,511	53	1,564	1,090
					-	1,122	1,122	1,654
		389,544			389,825	26,276	416,101	358,540
					-	45	45	50
18,984			39,223		58,207	40,443	98,650	87,434
73,286			129,877		203,163	275,438	478,601	445,930
265,635					265,635		265,635	260,194
186,463			92,353		278,816	6,613	285,429	265,295
59					59	115	174	312
12,420			45,579		57,999	12,586	70,585	101,571
564					564		564	564
(142,362)					(142,362)	(119,369)	(261,731)	(233,727)
				118,686	118,686		118,686	122,954
				354,403	354,403		354,403	309,923
				1,835	1,835		1,835	196
				26,308	26,308		26,308	25,069
				58,661	58,661		58,661	61,020
$ 469,713	$ -	$ 731,643	$ 307,032	$ 559,893	$ 2,395,968	$ 376,294	$ 2,772,262	$ 2,718,068
$ 11,007	$	$ 2,191	$	$	$ 39,650	$ 6,628	$ 46,278	$ 51,821
3,201					28,907	15	28,922	27,523
					-	4,665	4,665	4,155

119

CITY OF MILWAUKEE
COMBINED BALANCE SHEET -
ALL FUND TYPES, ACCOUNT GROUPS AND DISCRETELY PRESENTED COMPONENT UNITS
DECEMBER 31, 1999
WITH COMPARATIVE TOTALS FOR DECEMBER 31, 1998
(Thousands of Dollars)

Exhibit 1 (Continued)

	Governmental Fund Types			
	General	Special Revenue	Debt Service	Capital Projects
Liabilities (Continued):				
Due to other funds	$ 699	$ 3,503	$ 2,121	$ 2,242
Due to primary government				
Due to component units				
Due to other governmental agencies		18		
Bonds and notes payable - current		1,850	5	1,133
General obligation debt payable - current				
Payable from Restricted Assets:				
Deferred compensation				
Deferred revenue	527	8,619	30,669	12,481
Bonds and notes payable				
General obligation debt				
Unfunded pension costs				
Unfunded compensated absences				
Unfunded claims and judgments				
Revenue bonds payable				
Advances from other funds				
Advances from other governmental agencies				13,253
Obligations under capital lease				
Other liabilities				
Total Liabilities	$ 41,012	$ 19,606	$ 32,795	$ 35,865
Fund Equity and Other Credits:				
Contributed capital	$	$	$	$
Investment in general fixed assets				
Retained Earnings:				
Unreserved				
Fund Balances:				
Reserved for debt service - 2000 (1999)		12,351	31,322	
Reserved for future retirement of general obligation debt		1,165	73,848	
Reserved for delinquent taxes receivable		7,716		
Reserved for encumbrances, prepaids, carryovers and advances	28,610	(1)		19,156
Reserved for inventory	6,454			213
Reserved for mortgage trust	281			
Reserved for environmental remediation	291			
Reserved for deferred compensation				
Reserved for tax stabilization - 2000 (1999)	11,250			
Reserved for tax stabilization - 2001 (2000) and subsequent years' budgets	18,137			
Unreserved:				
Special assessment (deficit)				
Undesignated				(12,384)
Total Fund Equity and Other Credits	$ 65,023	$ 21,231	$ 105,170	$ 6,985
Total Liabilities, Fund Equity and Other Credits	$ 106,035	$ 40,837	$ 137,965	$ 42,850

The notes to the financial statements are an integral part of this statement.

Exhibit 1 (Continued)

| | Proprietary Fund Types | Fiduciary Fund Type | Account Groups | | Totals (Memorandum Only) | | Totals (Memorandum Only) Reporting Entity | |
Enterprise	Internal Service	Trust and Agency	General Fixed Assets	General Long-Term Obligations	Primary Government	Component Units	1999	1998 (Restated)
$ 7,031	$	$	$	$	$ 15,596	$ 1,738	$ 17,334	$ 32,904
					-	13,751	13,751	15,953
					18		18	377
		71,969			74,957	16,543	91,500	107,142
					-	2,330	2,330	3,819
8,948					8,948		8,948	7,646
					-		-	327,443
87		158,769			211,152	4,663	215,815	221,404
		100,000			100,000	1,939	101,939	113,206
77,942				473,089	551,031		551,031	510,857
				1,835	1,835		1,835	196
				26,308	26,308		26,308	25,069
				58,661	58,661		58,661	61,020
16,773					16,773	19,945	36,718	30,914
					13,253		13,253	10,979
					-	2,186	2,186	2,951
					-		-	145
					-	5,352	5,352	4,174
$ 124,989	$ -	$ 332,929	$ -	$ 559,893	$ 1,147,089	$ 79,755	$ 1,226,844	$ 1,559,698
$ 118,410	$	$	$	$	$ 118,410	$ 258,056	$ 376,466	$ 357,361
			307,032		307,032		307,032	293,798
226,314					226,314	38,483	264,797	287,865
					43,673		43,673	36,029
					75,013		75,013	86,925
					7,716		7,716	7,525
					47,765		47,765	49,764
					6,667		6,667	6,382
					281		281	281
					291		291	319
		389,544			389,544		389,544	
					11,250		11,250	12,820
					18,137		18,137	26,424
					(12,384)		(12,384)	(11,534)
		9,170			9,170		9,170	4,411
$ 344,724	$ -	$ 398,714	$ 307,032	$ -	$ 1,248,879	$ 296,539	$ 1,545,418	$ 1,158,370
$ 469,713	$ -	$ 731,643	$ 307,032	$ 559,893	$ 2,395,968	$ 376,294	$ 2,772,262	$ 2,718,068

COMBINED STATEMENT OF REVENUES, EXPENDITURES AND CHANGES IN FUND BALANCES -
ALL GOVERNMENTAL FUND TYPES AND EXPENDABLE TRUST FUNDS
FOR THE YEAR ENDED DECEMBER 31, 1999
WITH COMPARATIVE TOTALS FOR THE YEAR ENDED DECEMBER 31, 1998
(Thousands of Dollars)

Exhibit 2

	General	Special Revenue
Revenues:		
Property taxes	$ 89,250	$
Other taxes	10,283	
Special assessments		
Licenses and permits	8,996	
Intergovernmental	277,884	58,952
Charges for services	37,598	
Fines and forfeits	17,694	
Other	9,032	922
Total Revenues	$ 450,737	$ 59,874
Expenditures:		
Current:		
General government	$ 132,231	$ 1,457
Public safety	205,717	9,852
Public works	91,817	4,051
Health	11,401	13,952
Culture and recreation	16,627	2,016
Conservation and development	7,271	27,620
Other		
Capital outlay		
Debt Service:		
Principal retirement		
Interest		
Total Expenditures	$ 465,064	$ 58,948
Excess of Revenues over (under) Expenditures	$ (14,327)	$ 926
Other Financing Sources (Uses):		
Proceeds of bonds and notes	$	$ 9,090
Operating transfers in	7,632	
Operating transfers out	(73)	(11,320)
Operating transfers to component units	(150)	
Contributions received	651	
Contributions used	(612)	
Total Other Financing Sources (Uses)	$ 7,448	$ (2,230)
Excess of Revenues and Other Sources over (under) Expenditures and Other Uses	$ (6,879)	$ (1,304)
Fund Balances - January 1	71,776	22,535
Residual Equity Transfers from Other Funds	163	
Residual Equity Transfers to Other Funds	(37)	
Fund Balances - December 31	$ 65,023	$ 21,231

The notes to the financial statements are an integral part of this statement.

Exhibit 2 (Continued)

	Governmental Fund Types		Fiduciary Fund Type	Totals (Memorandum Only) Reporting Entity	
	Debt Service	Capital Projects	Expendable Trust	1999	1998 (Restated)
	$ 57,885	$ 13,791	$	$ 160,926	$ 152,715
	835			11,118	12,834
		3,362		3,362	4,180
				8,996	8,112
		5,889		342,725	341,196
				37,598	27,727
				17,694	16,138
	14,214	8,515	89,207	121,890	64,565
	$ 72,934	$ 31,557	$ 89,207	$ 704,309	$ 627,467
	$ 3	$	$	$ 133,691	$ 67,590
				215,569	260,630
				95,868	111,069
				25,353	34,436
				18,643	22,733
				34,891	33,009
			22,427	22,427	11,773
		100,922		100,922	101,222
	66,925			66,925	67,962
	22,640			22,640	21,024
	$ 89,568	$ 100,922	$ 22,427	$ 736,929	$ 731,448
	$ (16,634)	$ (69,365)	$ 66,780	$ (32,620)	$ (103,981)
	$	$ 74,222	$	$ 83,312	$ 99,680
	26,044	4,230	69	37,975	47,012
	(16,702)	(7,225)		(35,320)	(42,843)
				(150)	(150)
				651	743
				(612)	(587)
	$ 9,342	$ 71,227	$ 69	$ 85,856	$ 103,855
	$ (7,292)	$ 1,862	$ 66,849	$ 53,236	$ (126)
	107,996	12,628	331,854	546,789	222,102
	7,505		11	7,679	5,705
	(3,039)	(7,505)		(10,581)	(8,335)
	$ 105,170	$ 6,985	$ 398,714	$ 597,123	$ 219,346

123

COMBINED STATEMENT OF REVENUES, EXPENDITURES AND CHANGES IN FUND BALANCE - BUDGET AND ACTUAL - GENERAL AND BUDGETED SPECIAL REVENUE FUND TYPES

FOR THE YEAR ENDED DECEMBER 31, 1999

(Thousands of Dollars)

	Amended Budget	Actual on Budgetary Basis	General Fund Variance - Favorable (Unfavorable)
Revenues:			
Property taxes	$ 89,250	$ 89,250	$
Other taxes	10,155	10,283	128
Licenses and permits	7,700	8,996	1,296
Intergovemmental	277,943	277,884	(59)
Charges for services	38,652	37,598	(1,054)
Fines and forfeits	16,772	17,694	922
Other	13,240	9,032	(4,208)
Total Revenues	$ 453,712	$ 450,737	$ (2,975)
Expenditures:			
Current:			
General government	$ 137,279	$ 132,231	$ 5,048
Public safety	207,139	205,717	1,422
Public works	89,920	91,817	(1,897)
Health	11,741	11,401	340
Culture and recreation	17,053	16,627	426
Conservation and development	7,959	7,271	688
Total Expenditures	$ 471,091	$ 465,064	$ 6,027
Excess of Revenues over (under) Expenditures	$ (17,379)	$ (14,327)	$ 3,052
Other Financing Sources (Uses):			
Proceeds of bonds and notes	$	$ 1,312	$ 1,312
Operating transfers in	7,478	7,632	154
Operating transfers out	(69)	(73)	(4)
Operating transfers to component units	(150)	(150)	
Contributions received	1,000	651	(349)
Contributions used	(890)	(612)	278
Use of fund balance - reserved for tax stabilization	12,820	12,820	
Total Other Financing Sources (Uses)	$ 20,189	$ 21,580	$ 1,391
Excess of Revenues and Other Sources over (under) Expenditures and Other Uses	$ 2,810	$ 7,253	$ 4,443
Fund Balances - January 1 (Excludes Reserved for Tax Stabilization)	58,956	58,956	
Residual Equity Transfers from Other Funds	308	163	(145)
Residual Equity Transfers to Other Funds	(228)	(37)	191
Fund Balances (Deficits) - December 31	$ 61,846	$ 66,335	$ 4,489

The notes to the financial statements are an integral part of this statement.

Exhibit 3 (Continued)

	Special Revenue Funds			Totals (Memorandum Only) Reporting Entity		
Amended Budget	Actual on Budgetary Basis	Variance - Favorable (Unfavorable)	Amended Budget	Actual on Budgetary Basis	Variance - Favorable (Unfavorable)	
$	$	$ -	$ 89,250	$ 89,250	$ -	
		-	10,155	10,283	128	
		-	7,700	8,996	1,296	
59,805	58,952	(853)	337,748	336,836	(912)	
		-	38,652	37,598	(1,054)	
		-	16,772	17,694	922	
		-	13,240	9,032	(4,208)	
$ 59,805	$ 58,952	$ (853)	$ 513,517	$ 509,689	$ (3,828)	
$ 1,457	$ 1,457	$ -	$ 138,736	$ 133,688	$ 5,048	
10,310	9,852	458	217,449	215,569	1,880	
4,051	4,051	-	93,971	95,868	(1,897)	
14,438	13,952	486	26,179	25,353	826	
2,022	2,016	6	19,075	18,643	432	
27,580	27,620	(40)	35,539	34,891	648	
$ 59,858	$ 58,948	$ 910	$ 530,949	$ 524,012	$ 6,937	
$ (53)	$ 4	$ 57	$ (17,432)	$ (14,323)	$ 3,109	
$	$	$ -	$ -	$ 1,312	$ 1,312	
		-	7,478	7,632	154	
		-	(69)	(73)	(4)	
		-	(150)	(150)	-	
		-	1,000	651	(349)	
		-	(890)	(612)	278	
		-	12,820	12,820	-	
$ -	$ -	$ -	$ 20,189	$ 21,580	$ 1,391	
$ (53)	$ 4	$ 57	$ 2,757	$ 7,257	$ 4,500	
52	52	-	59,008	59,008	-	
		-	308	163	(145)	
	(57)	(57)	(228)	(94)	134	
$ (1)	$ (1)	$ -	$ 61,845	$ 66,334	$ 4,489	

Exhibit 4

CITY OF MILWAUKEE
COMBINED STATEMENT OF REVENUES, EXPENSES AND CHANGES IN RETAINED EARNINGS -
ALL PROPRIETARY FUND TYPES AND DISCRETELY PRESENTED COMPONENT UNITS
FOR THE YEAR ENDED DECEMBER 31, 1999
WITH COMPARATIVE TOTALS FOR THE YEAR ENDED DECEMBER 31, 1998
(Thousands of Dollars)

	Enterprise
Operating Revenues:	
Charges for services	$ 112,259
Operating Expenses:	
Milwaukee Metropolitan Sewerage District charges	$ 27,144
Employee services	7,258
Administrative and general	6,237
Housing assistance payments	
Depreciation	11,100
Transmission and distribution	15,662
Maintenance and utilities	
Services, supplies and materials	10,603
Payment in lieu of taxes	7,952
Water treatment	7,443
Water pumping	5,346
Billing and collection	3,527
Bad debts	
Interest expense and subsidies	
Cost of goods disbursed	
Rehabilitation costs (cost recoveries)	
Show expenses	
Other operating expenses	
Total Operating Expenses	$ 102,272
Operating Income (Loss)	$ 9,987
Nonoperating Revenues (Expenses):	
Federal grants and subsidies	$
Interest income	1,413
Interest expense	(4,023)
Loss on early repayments of Tax Incremental Districts	
Net gain (loss) on sale of fixed assets	
Contributions	
Other	(5,677)
Total Nonoperating Revenues (Expenses)	$ (8,287)
Income (Loss) before Operating Transfers	$ 1,700
Operating Transfers In	9,228
Operating Transfers Out	(11,883)
Operating Transfers from Primary Government	
Net Income (Loss)	$ (955)
Retained Earnings - January 1	227,269
Residual Equity Transfer to Other Funds	
Retained Earnings - December 31	$ 226,314

The notes to the financial statements are an integral part of this statement.

Exhibit 4 (Continued)

Internal Service	Totals (Memorandum Only) Primary Government	Component Units	Totals (Memorandum Only) Reporting Entity 1999	1998 (Restated)
$ 6,423	$ 118,682	$ 22,796	$ 141,478	$ 141,489
$	$ 27,144	$	$ 27,144	$ 31,205
3,821	11,079	582	11,661	12,388
	6,237	21,510	27,747	28,865
	.	16,819	16,819	18,052
139	11,239	24,325	35,564	13,300
	15,662		15,662	16,814
	.	12,513	12,513	12,515
2,179	12,782	91	12,873	12,339
	7,952		7,952	7,949
	7,443		7,443	7,667
	5,346		5,346	5,676
	3,527		3,527	3,414
	-	(325)	(325)	401
	-	102	102	120
643	643		643	78
	-	5,179	5,179	1,643
	-	181	181	304
	-	1,880	1,880	2,938
$ 6,782	$ 109,054	$ 82,857	$ 191,911	$ 175,668
$ (359)	$ 9,628	$(60,061)	$ (50,433)	$ (34,179)
$	$ -	$ 35,916	$ 35,916	$ 35,805
	1,413	5,573	6,986	6,256
(16)	(4,039)	(1,384)	(5,423)	(4,400)
		(4,119)	(4,119)	
20	20	(1,011)	(991)	(2,003)
	.	1,416	1,416	346
	(5,677)	1,770	(3,907)	2,403
$ 4	$ (8,283)	$ 38,161	$ 29,878	$ 38,407
$ (355)	$ 1,345	$(21,900)	$ (20,555)	$ 4,228
	9,228		9,228	7,668
	(11,883)		(11,883)	(11,837)
	.	150	150	150
$ (355)	$ (1,310)	$(21,750)	$ (23,060)	$ 209
363	227,632	60,233	287,865	287,656
(8)	(8)		(8)	-
$ -	$ 226,314	$ 38,483	$ 264,797	$ 287,865

CITY OF MILWAUKEE
COMBINED STATEMENT OF CASH FLOWS -
ALL PROPRIETARY FUND TYPES AND DISCRETELY PRESENTED COMPONENT UNITS
FOR THE YEAR ENDED DECEMBER 31, 1999
WITH COMPARATIVE TOTALS FOR THE YEAR ENDED DECEMBER 31, 1998
(Thousands of Dollars)

Exhibit 5

	Enterprise
CASH FLOWS FROM OPERATING ACTIVITIES:	
Operating income (loss)	$ 9,987
Adjustments to Reconcile Operating Income (Loss) to Cash Provided by (Used for) Operating Activities:	
Depreciation	11,100
Bad debt expense	
Loss on properties	
Other nonoperating revenues (expenses)	192
(Increase) decrease in receivables	(1,114)
(Increase) decrease in due from other funds	(182)
(Increase) decrease in due from primary government	
(Increase) decrease in due from other governmental agencies	
(Increase) decrease in inventory of materials and supplies	(308)
(Increase) decrease in inventory of property for resale	
(Increase) decrease in prepaid items	228
(Increase) decrease in other assets	(481)
Increase (decrease) in accounts payable	(5,648)
Increase (decrease) in accrued wages	373
Increase (decrease) in accrued expenses	
Increase (decrease) in due to other funds	(6,463)
Increase (decrease) in due to primary government	
Increase (decrease) in due to other governmental agencies	
Increase (decrease) in deferred revenue	(2)
Increase (decrease) in other liabilities	
Net Cash Provided by (Used for) Operating Activities	$ 7,682
CASH FLOWS FROM NONCAPITAL FINANCING ACTIVITIES:	
Operating transfers (to) from other funds	$ (2,862)
Other nonoperating revenues (expenses)	(5,869)
Increase (decrease) in due to other funds	(1,046)
Contributions	
Proceeds from bonds and notes payable	
Retirement of bonds and notes payable	
Repayments to primary government	
Payment on advance from other governmental agencies	
Net decrease (increase) in due to other governmental units	
Loss on early repayment of Tax Incremental Districts	
Operating transfer from primary government	
Residual equity transfer to (from) component unit	
Net Cash Provided by (Used for) Noncapital Financing Activities	$ (9,777)
CASH FLOWS FROM CAPITAL AND RELATED FINANCING ACTIVITIES:	
Capital contributions	$ 4,540
Proceeds from sale of bonds and notes	8,133
Proceeds from sale of revenue bonds	12,686
Acquisition of property, plant and equipment	(30,279)
Retirement of revenue bonds payable	
Retirement of bonds and notes payable	
Retirement of general obligation debt	
Interest paid	(7,645)
Sale of land and other assets	(4,030)

Exhibit 5 (Continued)

Internal Service	Totals (Memorandum Only) Primary Government	Component Units	Totals (Memorandum Only) Reporting Entity 1999	Totals (Memorandum Only) Reporting Entity 1998 (Restated)
$ (359)	$ 9,628	$ (60,061)	$ (50,433)	$ (34,179)
139	11,239	24,325	35,564	13,300
	•	(325)	(325)	401
	•	868	868	158
	192		192	296
109	(1,005)	600	(405)	(4,743)
	(182)	(385)	(567)	(140)
	•	359	359	(377)
		(866)	(866)	898
65	(243)	(13)	(256)	(380)
	•	(4,489)	(4,489)	(653)
	228	1,586	1,814	(2,368)
	(481)	7	(474)	(137)
(263)	(5,911)	391	(5,520)	(9,225)
(318)	55	1	56	121
	•	510	510	(350)
	(6,463)	385	(6,078)	(7,887)
	•	990	990	6,202
		3,606	3,606	329
(57)	(59)	(287)	(346)	1,271
	•	1,243	1,243	(229)
$ (684)	$ 6,998	$ (31,555)	$ (24,557)	$ (37,692)
$	$ (2,862)	$	$ (2,862)	$ (2,404)
	(5,869)	7,087	1,218	3,790
	(1,046)	30,976	29,930	1,033
	-		-	34,034
		351	351	39
		(693)	(693)	(167)
		(3,210)	(3,210)	286
				(276)
				(763)
		(4,119)	(4,119)	
		150	150	150
	•		-	572
$ -	$ (9,777)	$ 30,542	$ 20,765	$ 36,294
$ 27	$ 4,567	$ 16,394	$ 20,961	$ 15,156
	8,133		8,133	24,869
	12,686		12,686	4,873
(31)	(30,310)	(1,637)	(31,947)	(60,251)
	-	(1,643)	(1,643)	(5,728)
	-	(18,868)	(18,868)	(924)
	(7,645)		(7,645)	(5,964)
(16)	(4,046)	(346)	(4,392)	(4,410)
	•		-	17

CITY OF MILWAUKEE
COMBINED STATEMENT OF CASH FLOWS -
ALL PROPRIETARY FUND TYPES AND DISCRETELY PRESENTED COMPONENT UNITS
FOR THE YEAR ENDED DECEMBER 31, 1999
WITH COMPARATIVE TOTALS FOR THE YEAR ENDED DECEMBER 31, 1998
(Thousands of Dollars)

Exhibit 5 (Continued)

	Enterprise
CASH FLOWS FROM CAPITAL AND RELATED FINANCING ACTIVITIES (Continued):	
Payment of obligation for capital lease	$
Return of contributions	(58)
Operating transfers to other funds	203
Residual equity transfer to other funds	
Repairs and restorations	(1,295)
Net advances to other funds	
(Increase) decrease in fiscal agent funds	
Proceeds from notes and loans receivable	
Payment of notes receivable	
Net Cash Provided by (Used for) Capital and Related Financing Activities	$ (17,745)
CASH FLOWS FROM INVESTING ACTIVITIES:	
Interest income	$ 1,413
Purchases of investments	
Proceeds from the sale and maturity of investments	6,000
New loans made	
Loan payments received	
(Increase) decrease in accrued interest	
Capital expenditures on properties	
Proceeds from the sale of properties	
Other	
Net Cash Provided by (Used for) Investing Activities	$ 7,413
Net Increase (Decrease) in Cash and Cash Equivalents	$ (12,427)
Cash and Cash Equivalents at January 1	32,512
Cash and Cash Equivalents at December 31	$ 20,085
Cash and Cash Equivalents at December 31 Consist of:	
Unrestricted cash	$ 20,085
Restricted cash	
	$ 20,085

Non-cash Activities:
Enterprise Funds:
The Port of Milwaukee disposed of fixed assets with a net value of $29 during the year.
During the year, water mains and related property, installed by others were deeded to the Water Works in the amount of $1,716.

Internal Service Fund:
The Central Services Fund was closed at year end, all assets and liabilities were transferred to the General Fund.

Component Units:
Pabst Theater recorded equipment purchases of $90 paid directly by the City of Milwaukee.
The Neighborhood Improvement Development Corporation received contributed capital in the form of Community Development Block Grant Loans in the amount of $268.

The notes to the financial statements are an integral part of this statement.

Exhibit 5 (Continued)

Internal Service	Totals (Memorandum Only) Primary Government	Component Units	Totals (Memorandum Only) Reporting Entity	
			1999	1998 (Restated)
$ (44)	$ (44)	$	$ (44)	$ (40)
(97)	(155)		(155)	(187)
	203		203	(1,765)
(8)	(8)		(8)	
	(1,295)		(1,295)	(2,055)
	-		-	1,146
	-	4,540	4,540	4,221
	-		-	(4,158)
	-		-	1,311
$(169)	$(17,914)	$ (1,560)	$ (19,474)	$ (33,889)
$	$ 1,413	$ 5,573	$ 6,986	$ 6,865
	-	(15,348)	(15,348)	(20,977)
	6,000	12,947	18,947	43,998
	-	(7,463)	(7,463)	(6,905)
	-	12,687	12,687	5,990
	-	(122)	(122)	37
	-	(1,363)	(1,363)	(1,636)
	-	991	991	1,680
	-	382	382	11
$ -	$ 7,413	$ 8,284	$ 15,697	$ 29,063
$ (853)	$(13,280)	$ 5,711	$ (7,569)	$ (6,224)
853	33,365	37,863	71,228	77,452
$ -	$ 20,085	$ 43,574	$ 63,659	$ 71,228
$	$ 20,085	$ 42,452	$ 62,537	$ 69,574
		1,122	1,122	1,654
$ -	$ 20,085	$ 43,574	$ 63,659	$ 71,228